Praise for Books by Stephen Mansfield

"I think this is a game-changing book. [A] really, really powerful book."

Glenn Beck

"This is an important book. . . . I wish everyone could have read this book ten years ago. At least read it now."

Eric Metaxas

"You will be thrilled, disturbed, and astounded, but ultimately inspired and uplifted."

Rabbi Daniel Lapin

"Every voter in the country should read this book!"

Dave Ramsey, *New York Times* bestselling author;
nationally syndicated radio show host

"You must read this perceptive and well-written book."

Archbishop Desmond Tutu

"Mansfield makes a persuasive case for why it's both important and appropriate to expect candidates for president of the United States to be open and detailed about their personal religious journeys and beliefs."

Jim Wallis, *New York Times* bestselling author;
president of Sojourners;
editor-in-chief of *Sojourners* magazine

"Stephen Mansfield's latest book takes on one of the most common points of contention in the news today: religion. He's demanding that candidates come clean on their beliefs before they get to the Oval Office. He's right, and he makes his case in a unique, fascinating manner that is rich in American history."

Brian Kilmeade, *FOX News*

"Mansfield's approach is neither partisan nor partial to a particular aspect of religion. Stephen Mansfield challenges both voters and the media to ask the right questions."

Dr. Joel C. Hunter, senior pastor of Northland Church

CHOOSING
DONALD
TRUMP

Also by Stephen Mansfield

The Character and Greatness of Winston Churchill:
Hero in Time of Crisis

Then Darkness Fled: The Liberating Wisdom of Booker T. Washington

Forgotten Founding Father: The Heroic Legacy of George Whitefield

The Faith of George W. Bush

The Faith of the American Soldier

Benedict XVI: His Life and Mission

The Faith of Barack Obama

The Search for God and Guinness

Lincoln's Battle with God

Killing Jesus

Mansfield's Book of Manly Men

The Miracle of the Kurds

CHOOSING DONALD TRUMP

God, Anger, Hope, and
Why Christian Conservatives Supported Him

STEPHEN MANSFIELD

BakerBooks
a division of Baker Publishing Group
Grand Rapids, Michigan

Published by Baker Books
a division of Baker Publishing Group
PO Box 6287, Grand Rapids, MI 49516-6287
www.bakerbooks.com

Printed in the United States of America

Library of Congress Cataloging-in-Publication Data is on file at the Library of Congress, Washington, DC.

978-0-8010-0733-0 (cloth)

17 18 19 20 21 22 23   7 6 5 4 3 2 1

To the Millennials
who are much maligned and much conflicted,
yet whose large souls and larger hopes
may yet lead us
to a greater America.

The church must be reminded that it is not the master or the servant of the state, but rather the conscience of the state. It must be the guide and the critic of the state, and never its tool.

If the church does not recapture its prophetic zeal, it will become an irrelevant social club without moral or spiritual authority. If the church does not participate actively in the struggle for peace and for economic and racial justice, it will forfeit the loyalty of millions and cause men everywhere to say that it has atrophied its will.

But if the church will free itself from the shackles of a deadening status quo, and, recovering its great historic mission, will speak and act fearlessly and insistently in terms of justice and peace, it will enkindle the imagination of mankind and fire the souls of men, imbuing them with a glowing and ardent love for truth, justice, and peace.

Martin Luther King Jr., "A Knock at Midnight"[1]

Contents

PART 4 OF PROPHETS AND PRESIDENTS

Introduction

I am the only one who can make America great again.

Donald Trump[1]

Politics is almost always a matter of choosing between holding your nose and holding your nose tighter, but the 2016 election that placed Donald Trump in the White House was a particularly pungent affair. Perhaps the offerings were simply exposed to the elements for too long. Perhaps this explains the spoilage and the rot that set in.

There had been the blistering primary battle between Hillary Clinton and Senator Bernie Sanders. It lasted for more than a year, required six bludgeoning debates, and when it was over had solved very little. Hillary Clinton was the Democratic Party nominee. No one was surprised.

The Republican primaries took an even greater toll. There were seventeen candidates, twelve debates, and nine forums to endure. The bloodletting threatened to never end. Civility abandoned the field. The word *gravitas* never came to mind. Candidates insulted each other's wives, publicly questioned their opponents' eternal salvation, accused each other's families of complicity in the Kennedy assassination, and disparaged each other in scatological terms. Hand size was an oft-used metaphor for size of another kind, and more than one candidate felt the need to assure the nation that he measured up to expectations.

When it was all over and the blood was wiped from television screens nationwide, Donald Trump was the Republican Party nominee for president of the United States.

He was the most unusual party nominee in American history. He had never held public office. He made his wealth and his reputation in cutthroat real estate deals and as an owner of gambling casinos. He specialized in breaking the rules. His campaign was one of the least orthodox, least disciplined, and least focused in US political history—and still he won his party's nomination handily.

The immorality of his prior life alone set him apart as an American presidential candidate. He had been married three times and publicly boasted of his marital infidelities. He had often been a guest of adult talk shows where he found it necessary to describe his favorite variations on traditional marital practices. Voters could watch it all on YouTube. During his campaign, he swore, he mocked the handicapped, he insulted nearly every ethnicity in the United States, and he was eager to expose the sins of his political rivals.

None of it did him harm. He seemed coated in invisible Teflon. Even a decade-old recording of him describing sexual conquests real and intended did him no lasting damage. He could not mangle a fact or lob an insult so as to hurt himself in the polls. He was bulletproof. He was untouchable. He became the forty-fifth president of the United States.

Yet none of this was as surprising as the support from religious Americans that Donald Trump commanded. At his side stood some of the most visible faith leaders in the nation. Famous preachers declared him God's man. Eminent theologians said he was chosen. Others said he was a Lincoln, perhaps not an orthodox believer but guided nevertheless by the better angels of his nature and the hand of a history-ruling God. A few even said he was a Churchill—crass, blasphemous, gifted, and ordained.

Trump gave back in kind. He swore to protect the Christian faith. He spoke of the religion of the political left as a religion alien to the good of the nation. He showed he had been doing his homework. He promised to "totally destroy" the Johnson Amendment that prevented clergy from supporting political causes and candidates. Few of his rivals even knew what it was. The much-maligned religious right knew, though, and realized in amazement that Donald Trump—of all people—had made himself a champion of their cause.

It was all part of a counterassault in a decades-old war between religious left and religious right. After the grand unity and patriotic fervor of World War II, the nation had begun to fray, pulled apart largely by competing religious visions. As early as 1947, the US Supreme Court ruled in *Everson v. Board of Education* that a strict wall of separation should exist between church and state. It was a wall that "must be kept high and impregnable," the esteemed justices said. They "could not approve the slightest breach."[2]

This had not been the intention of the founding fathers when they drafted their First Amendment. Nor had it been the experience of generations of Americans. It meant, though, that prayer in public schools, Ten Commandments posted on courthouse walls, crosses in federal cemeteries, Bibles in classrooms, and even the very existence of military chaplains—indeed, nearly any appearance of religion in American public life—were about to be targeted by a new and activist secularism and by a religious left that said grace over it all.

It was only the beginning of upheavals. Between the Supreme Court's 1947 *Everson* case and its 1973 *Roe v. Wade* decision legalizing abortion, the United States experienced a sexual revolution, an influential counterculture movement, an influx of non-Judeo/Christian religions, a questioning of the Vietnam War that led in turn to a questioning of national purpose, and a growing distrust of governing officials inspired by the agonizing Watergate scandals. It seemed to millions of Americans that both God and country were under siege.

By the late 1970s, these same Americans believed a counter-insurgency was required. It was time to restore what had been lost. This began with the rise of Jerry Falwell, a faith-based march called Washington for Jesus in 1980, and the advent of the Moral Majority. Ronald Reagan led the troops in those days, assisted by religious broadcasters James Dobson, Pat Robertson, and the eminent D. James Kennedy. They would return America to God. They would see the forces of secularism held in check. They would renew the purposes of the founding fathers. The movement did much to shape the nation. Though the later ascent of Bill Clinton meant some reversals for the strengthening religious right, the presidency of George W. Bush worked to restore what had been lost.

It was Barack Obama who took up the fallen standard of the religious left. In his 2004 Democratic National Convention speech in Boston, he declared, "We worship an awesome God in the Blue States." It was a trumpet call of faith, an opening salvo in a battle to retake the moral high ground in American politics. It helped carry Obama into the White House in 2008 and gave the nation a presidency devoted to the ideals of the faith-based political left.

Traditional, conservative Americans were forced to watch over the next eight years while the Obama administration attempted a religious redefinition of the American experience. The president repeatedly insisted the nation was no longer Christian. He worked to redefine marriage, redefine acceptable sexual ethics, redefine the nation's understanding of when human life begins, redefine the basis of public morality—indeed, redefine American history itself. His administration thought nothing of suing traditional Christians for following the dictates of their faith or making them suffer for attempting to honor ancient moral boundaries. Each of these incursions upon religious liberty was championed by a confident president ever quoting the Bible in support of his views.

By the dawn of the 2016 presidential race, religious conservatives were traumatized by the Obama years and fearful a second Clinton presidency would mean more of the same. They would back anyone who could win. They would take a nonbeliever. They would accept a candidate of doubtful morality. They were even willing to risk racial and gender offense on the part of their candidate. They could not endure more years of bombardment from a religious left intent upon remaking the nation.

So they stood with Donald Trump, and in so doing they took responsibility for the Trump presidency before the nation and the world. They "own" him now. They are wed to him, whatever he does. They will be made to answer for the mores, the methods, and the machinations of the Trump administration. They will never be allowed to forget that they are in part responsible for placing the name Trump alongside names such as Washington and Lincoln, Roosevelt and Reagan.

They have taken a great risk, these religious conservatives. A war over political morality is being fought in the United States today. It is better understood as a battle of religious visions, for law is religion codified just as culture is religion externalized. In this war, religious conservatives have chosen Donald Trump as their civil champion. If he serves them well, their cause may endure as a defining influence upon the course of American history. If he fails, if he gives in to his lesser nature and betrays their vision, the banner of religious conservatives may be forced from the field of cultural battle for a generation or more. These are the stakes at risk, and this is how much Americans of traditional religious values have invested in Donald Trump.

This book is about that investment. It is not primarily a biography or an electoral history. It is instead about the faith that has shaped Donald Trump, about the religious factors that played a role in his election, about what religious conservatives have risked in supporting Donald Trump, and about what religion may mean in a Trump administration.

This book is also about a generation of Americans at war with themselves over the meaning of God to the American experience. It is a war that continues to tear the nation at its seams, as it has for more than a generation, and that threatens to permanently taint a young generation on the rise. We will not see this war concluded during the Trump years, but we will see it redefined either by the faith-based victories of the Trump administration or by the embarrassment of its failures and betrayals to the cause of religion. Either way, the Trump presidency could become among the most religiously decisive in American history.

PART 1

An Unlikely Champion

In the 2016 election, Donald Trump ran for president against a Baptist minister, two sons of pastors, and a slate of Republican candidates, most of whom considered themselves evangelicals. He then ran against one of the most vocally religious Democrats in the country. He was among the least religious and least religiously articulate men ever to run for the presidency. And he won. He did it with the surprising help of a vast majority of the nation's religious conservatives. They have taken responsibility for him now, and this may, in time, exact a very dear price.

1 Convergence

> I think people are shocked when they find out that I am a
> Christian, that I am a religious person. They see me with all
> the surroundings of wealth so they sometimes don't associate
> that with being religious. That's not accurate. I go to church. I
> love God, and I love having a relationship with Him.
>
> Donald Trump[1]

It was September 24, 2012, and Donald Trump was scheduled to
speak at a convocation of Liberty University in Lynchburg, Virginia.
This was the largest Protestant university in the world. Trump knew
it and wanted to impress. He had considered a presidential run earlier
in the year but thought it ill-timed, yet knew there would come a day
when he would declare himself a candidate. It was important that he
make himself known to the more than ten thousand students present and the tens of thousands more watching online. As important
were the millions of evangelicals around the country who would
eventually take note of his thirty-minute speech.

Trump was introduced by President Jerry Falwell Jr., son of the
university's founder, as "one of the greatest visionaries of our time."
The rest of the lengthy introduction could have been given at a real

estate convention. Trump's luxurious properties, his philanthropy, and his rising media empire were all extolled. President Falwell drew cheers from the students when he announced that the school planned to replace some of its dormitories and that perhaps a Trump Tower might adorn the campus one day. Falwell was, as most university presidents are, nothing if not a salesman.

The speech was classic Donald Trump. He honored the memory of Jerry Falwell Sr., founder of the school, and thrilled students by acknowledging that learning about God is more important than having all the business knowledge in the world. He then criticized America's leaders, warned of America's future, and couldn't stay away from the theme of the nation's "idiot politicians."

In typical style, Trump pushed the boundaries of propriety. While giving a list of steps for success—some as innocuous as "Work hard" and "Love what you do"—he also told the students to "Get even" with those who wronged them, to never "Let people take advantage of you," and to "Get a prenuptial." Then he added, "But these are the things I can't say at Liberty." The comment drew howling laughter. The speech was a success. The students gave Trump a prolonged and adoring standing ovation.

What few of those in attendance could have known was the intense effort Trump had devoted to one part of his speech in particular. He wanted to show his Christian credentials. He wanted to assure that he belonged among these evangelical students, that he, too, was a man of faith. So he asked the university to prepare a slide to be shown during his talk. It was a photograph of a young Donald Trump on the day of his baptism, along with a baptismal certificate confirming that the all-important deed had been done.

It was a simple request and the university happily agreed. That should have been the end of it. Like any university, Liberty was experienced with Keynote and PowerPoint presentations. In their convocation, even the song lyrics for worship are projected on huge screens. Millions of such images have been shown during classroom lectures and student presentations in the school's history. A single slide would be no problem.

The matter just wouldn't go away. Donald Trump was obsessed. There were repeated calls to university officials—and not by executive assistants or public relations staff. The calls came from Trump himself. And often. He worried that the school had the right photo and that they would highlight it just as he wished. He wanted to know if his face could be emphasized so that the audience would know which child in the photo he was. Could the certificate be read? Was it all clear enough? Would it appear at the right time in his talk?[2]

The memory of these calls prompted laughter from university officials long after Trump's 2012 talk. There was more in this, though, than a nervous speaker concerned about the state of his visual aids. Trump was eager for religious conservatives to know that he was not what they had been told. He was not merely the unforgiving mogul with the morally questionable past. He was also the freckle-faced boy who had been confirmed in his faith at First Presbyterian Church, Jamaica, Queens. He was a man who had sat in church by the hour to hear the revered Norman Vincent Peale preach, and he had made the eminent preacher/statesman's methods his own. He had come to love many of the nation's leading religious broadcasters. He watched them late into the night, sometimes on obscure cable channels, and was not beyond calling them when moved by something they said.

Yet he was clumsy in matters of religion, largely because he had worn the garment of his Christianity loosely throughout his life, and usually only when fashionable. It was why he did not know that the evangelical students and faculty at Liberty University would not be won by a Presbyterian baptismal certificate from sixty years ago. They wanted a conversion story, heartfelt and tearful and reminiscent of revivals past. They wanted "fruit," evidence of a life changed by conversion and modeled on the message of Jesus Christ. They would know that getting even with enemies in business was the opposite of what Jesus had taught. They believed that prenuptial agreements and multiple marriages and sexual conquests tallied like wild game bagged on safari were part of the scourge of their generation. Trump did not know these things or, if he did, was unwilling to distance himself from the offense.

Still, there was something remarkable and sincere about Trump's eagerness to be accepted by religious conservatives. It is true that he had political aspirations. He never hid this. He wanted their support and knew that to get it he would have to show sympathy for their concerns. He lived in a transactional world. A man got only as good as he gave. He expected to pay up for privileges given, for access and power provided. This was the world of Donald Trump, and he expected it to be no different in matters of religion and politics.

Yet he had a tender place in his heart for men and women who taught religious truth. He admired them. He was in awe of their power and moved by their gifts for helping people become more than they had been. His own life had been profoundly shaped by Norman Vincent Peale, the pastor of Marble Collegiate Church in New York and the founder of a religious empire built on the principles captured in his epic bestseller, *The Power of Positive Thinking.* For many an hour Trump had listened to Peale as he spoke of the example of Jesus, of the grace God gave to live a better life, and of the battles to be fought against godless communism and the secularism of the age.

"He would instill a very positive feeling about God that also made me feel positive about myself," Trump would say later. "I would literally leave that church feeling like I could listen to another three sermons."[3]

It is hard to exaggerate the impact of Peale upon Donald Trump's life. From the time his family made the move from First Presbyterian Church to Peale's Marble Collegiate Church in 1975, Peale and his teachings were interwoven with Trump's life and business. Peale officiated at his first wedding, conducted the funeral services for both of his parents, and was the honored clergyman at birthdays, wedding anniversaries, births, and even building dedications.

Perhaps more, Peale was the spiritual father who filled gaps left by the demanding, hard-driving biological father with whom Donald Trump had to contend. It was Peale who told Trump he was the famous preacher's "greatest student of all time."[4] It was Peale who wrote to congratulate him on the opening of Trump Tower and said he had always believed "you were going to be America's greatest builder." In fact, he said, "You have already arrived at that status and believe me, as your friend, I am very proud of you."[5]

These were sentiments sure to capture the heart of a son whose natural father "freely dispensed criticism, but rarely praise."[6] Peale became the loving mentor and father figure that Fred Trump, Donald's father, could never be. This meant that Donald Trump was drawn ever more deeply into the "thought process" of Peale's theology. It has done much to shape the Donald Trump of today, as we shall see. Peale believed, for example, that "attitudes are more important than facts." His book titles alone express the pillars of his teaching: *You Can Win*, *Guide to Confident Living*, *You Can If You Think You Can*, *Enthusiasm Makes the Difference*, and, of course, *The Power of Positive Thinking*.

Trump drank in Peale's system, and it left him both with a love for dynamic clergy and with a theology to match his ambitions. As one biographer has written of Donald Trump and his father:

> As nearly perfect practitioners of the power of positive thinking, they both wanted to achieve the kind of wealth and status that would elevate them above other men. In Peale they found a pastor who taught them that God wanted the same thing for them and that the "infinite forces of the universe" were available to them if only they used positive thinking and trained their minds "to think victory."[7]

This meant, then, that when Trump spoke at Liberty University in 2012, and certainly four years later when he ran for the Oval Office, he was a man churched if not yet converted, intrigued if not yet convinced, eager if not yet captured by a transforming faith in God. The minister who knew his spiritual life at the time better than anyone outside of his family said that Trump was spiritually "hungry."[8]

If this is true, then it means that Trump's association with the nation's leading ministers during his 2016 presidential campaign might have led to profound change for him and, ultimately, to a nobler president for the country. They might have called him to a more orthodox and full-bodied belief system than he had received under Norman Vincent Peale. They might have challenged him about some of his extreme behavior. When he swore, they might have reminded him of his younger listeners. When he called for violence against protestors or went on racist rants or spoke of women in disparaging terms, they might have reminded him of the example of Jesus and helped him recover his moral balance. They might also have whispered in his ear from time to time, "Always remember the poor."

In short, had they maintained prophetic distance, had they been more interested in urging the candidate toward God and his ways and less interested in allying themselves to power at any moral cost, great good might have been done.

It was largely not to be.

National religious leaders often seemed more interested in anointing Donald Trump than in challenging him or calling him to his best. A prime example of this occurred when Trump spoke at Liberty University a second time, in January 2016. By this time, he had achieved what he set out to accomplish in 2012. He had made himself familiar to religious conservatives. He had proven himself a man at least friendly to the Christian faith. After eight years of Barack Obama and facing a possible eight more under Hillary Clinton, many Americans heard Trump's promise to defend religious liberty with grateful ears. National religious leaders welcomed him with open arms.

Some went even further.

President Jerry Falwell Jr.'s introduction at that second Liberty University speech came close to portraying Trump as the ideal Christian. The university president quoted Matthew 7:16—"You shall know them by their fruit"—and said that Trump's life displayed the fruit described in this passage. He recounted as evidence that Trump had generously rescued a Harlem basketball program and saved Newton, Iowa, from the devastation of its main business moving to Mexico. He told the tale of Trump paying the mortgage of a family that had helped when his limousine broke down by the side of a road. He also offered the fact that Trump's staff loved him.

Falwell said he had attended the Republican debate in Charleston the previous week and that Trump was the only candidate who shook hands and posed for pictures afterward. This, he suggested, was a sign of Trump's kindness to strangers. "In my opinion," Falwell said, "Trump lives a life of loving and helping others as Jesus taught in the Great Commandment."[9] The candidate was not unlike Reagan, who was condemned by religious leaders as a Hollywood actor and a divorced man. Those leaders preferred the Baptist Sunday school teacher Jimmy Carter. "He may have been a great Sunday school teacher," Falwell said, "but look what happened to our nation while he was president."

The young university president declared that Trump was much like his own father, Jerry Falwell Sr. The elder Falwell was a generous man. He was a courageous man. He loved his enemies and was kind to his political opponents. He was also fierce in defense of the truth. He had once put a sign in front of the school that read, "Politically Incorrect Since 1971." All of this described Donald Trump as well, a man whom Falwell said he had introduced in 2012 as "the greatest visionary of our time." It was still true.

Trump had asked for none of this, we should remember. He had not declared himself an ideal Christian. He did not describe himself in glowing terms using the words of Jesus. He had not asked the president of Liberty University to compare him to Jesus Christ, Jerry Falwell Sr., Martin Luther King Jr., or Ronald Reagan. Nor, in the months to come, would he ask the revered Christian psychologist

Dr. James Dobson to tweet that he knew the minister who helped Trump become born again. He would also not ask Dr. Robert Jeffress of First Baptist Church in Dallas to declare that Trump might be the most faith-friendly president in American history. He would not ask that religious leaders nationwide excuse his excesses, pardon his sins, or portray him in divinely ordained terms before American voters. He had instead simply said he was a Christian, that he had long attended church, and that he would defend Christianity since it was so much under attack in the world.

This reticence to urge him toward a broader faith and deeper character was unfortunate, particularly given a feature of Trump's personality: he likes being challenged by people he trusts. He admits that he tests people when opportunity allows. He asks the probing question. He may even pick a low-grade fight. He does it to get a sense of a person's mettle. He likes it when the same is done to him—again, by people he trusts and who intend only to make him better. He is ever the competitor, and true competitors always welcome being spurred to their best by a committed teammate. The religious leaders who surrounded him in the 2016 campaign might have been just such teammates, had they been willing to take the risk of calling him to a more vibrant Christian faith.

It is not an opportunity irretrievably lost, though. These same leaders will have access to this president for years to come.

The broader matter of import is this: there was a convergence in 2016, one that will shape the nation for many years. A Christian-friendly but deeply flawed Donald Trump won support from religious leaders terrified by Hillary Clinton. Then both these religious leaders and Trump appealed to a largely white, largely middle class, and largely conservative Christian anger that empowered Trump to capture the White House. The impact of this convergence will be felt for generations. Understanding it is the beginning of repairing the damage done and rebuilding what must be rebuilt.

# 2 | Mixture

No one reads the Bible more than I do.

Donald Trump[1]

On June 16, 2015, Donald Trump declared his candidacy for president of the United States. It was a Tuesday. The previous Sunday, he had celebrated his sixty-ninth birthday.

It was, as expected, a tightly scripted event. A crowd of hundreds filled the lobby of Trump Tower on Fifth Avenue in New York. Flags and star-spangled bunting adorned nearly every available surface. The Trump name, in huge, shiny letters, rose imposingly above it all.

The festivities began with Ivanka Trump stepping to the podium. She is often handed the role of both framing and explaining her father. She has a calm demeanor and seems perhaps more centered and somewhat more intelligent than the rest of her gathered clan. For five minutes she extolled all that Donald Trump had accomplished in his life and all that he would achieve for the American people if they would but give him a chance.

The introduction made, the sound system began blaring Neil Young's "Rockin' in the Free World." It was an anomaly. While the chorus of this classic seems to cheer the freedom of rock and roll blaring wildly in the western world, the verses are more subdued. They warn of devastations to come and describe the human tragedies of modern life.

This meaning was lost to the exhilarated crowd at Trump Tower, though, for the candidate had begun to descend. In his trademark dark blue suit, white shirt, and ruby tie, Donald Trump rode the grand escalator in the lobby of his building to its main floor, holding the hand of his wife, Melania, who was trimly dressed in white. Had the occasion not been the launch of a presidential campaign, it might easily have passed for a wedding or a welcome for visiting royalty.

A Trump speech followed. It was all that Americans have since come to expect. The man who had already declared himself the "most successful person ever to run for the presidency, by far," announced the death of the American dream, that losers have been running the country, his own intention to make the nation great again, and his certainty that he, as a man who is "really rich," can be the "truly great leader" America needs.[2]

The crowd cheered. The cameras honed in. It was a successful launch. Donald Trump's disciplined team, his spectacular building, his handsome family, and his practiced call to arms won the day.

There would be other events equally scripted and just as effective in the months to come. Yet an important question arises from them all: If Team Trump was as capable as they evidently were of crafting meaningful moments and placing their candidate in just the right setting for just the right impact, why, then, was Donald Trump so stunningly inept when dealing with religion in the 2016 campaign?

He had declared for office before. Since then, he had watched every race for the White House with the unflinching gaze of a tiger eyeing its prey. He had to know that religion would surface again and again during his campaign. He had to know that he would be asked about every matter of spiritual import from his mother's prayers to his church attendance to the guilt he felt at the first stirrings of boyhood lust.

Even if the candidate had no sense of the religious land mines lining his path to the White House, there were people paid to know. Faith has been an increasingly contentious issue in presidential campaigns for decades. It is why directors of faith outreach are hired and why consultants are brought in early to school the candidate in all matters remotely relating to deity.

None of this seemed of concern to the Trump campaign. The candidate spoke of religion as though he were a visitor from Mars. It was hard to watch.

Just before the New York State primary, a radio host asked Trump if there was a favorite Bible verse or story that inspired him. "Well, I think many," the candidate replied, taking a big breath to stall for time.

> I mean, when we get into the Bible, I think many, so many. And some people—look, an eye for an eye, you can almost say that. That's not a particularly nice thing. But you know, if you look at what's happening to our country, I mean, when you see what's going on with our country, how people are taking advantage of us . . . we have to be firm and have to be very strong. And we can learn a lot from the Bible, that I can tell you.[3]

It could, surprisingly, get worse. Asked by Fox News about his faith, he answered, "I'm a Protestant. I'm a Presbyterian. Very important. I'm also busy and probably busier than I should be. But I am a Christian. I'm a Protestant. I'm Presbyterian."[4] When political consultant and pollster Frank Luntz asked him if God helped him in business, he replied, "God helped me by giving me a certain brain, whether that's a good thing or a bad thing."[5] When Luntz asked him if there is anyone in the Bible he looked up to, he said, "Nobody that I would compare to."[6] Asked about who God is to him, he spoke at length about buying a golf course.

He seemed to have floated above a life of faith rather than actually lived one. He was completely without details from the journey, without the familiarities that naturally belong to a person of sincere religion.

He could not name a favorite Bible verse or even which portion of the Bible—the Old Testament or the New—he preferred. He had not attended church regularly since his favorite preacher retired in the mid-1980s. It showed. In an Iowa church, he confused a communion plate with an offering plate and almost put money on top of cups of wine. He told an interviewer he had never asked forgiveness of God but would as soon as he did something wrong. He said he tries "not to bring God into that picture."[7]

Then he rethought this answer:

> Now, when I take—you know, when we go in church and when I drink my little wine, which is about the only wine I drink, and have my little cracker, I guess that is a form of asking for forgiveness. And I do that as often as possible, because I feel cleansed, ok? But, you know, to me that is important, I do that. In terms of officially—see, I could tell you absolutely, and everybody—I don't think in terms of that. I think in terms of, let's go on and let's make it right.[8]

He was invited to commend a community program at a Detroit church but opened fire against Hillary Clinton so viciously that the church's pastor had to shut him down.[9] He once told a roomful of Jewish Republicans, "I'm a negotiator, like you folks. . . . You're not going to support me because I don't want your money."[10] He tweeted that comments by Pope Francis were "disgraceful."[11] He freely admitted that he goes to church mainly on Christmas and Easter because he is busy.

It was, in short, the worst presentation of religion by a presidential candidate in recent memory. Donald Trump either had a faith he could not articulate and knew little about or he was faking religion for political gain. Either way, he was clumsy at best and duplicitous at worst in matters of religion. This is particularly surprising given that much of the Trump campaign strategy involved portraying the candidate as a champion of religious liberty, as a defender of mainstream faith. It seems someone should have taken him aside and prepared him for the role.

Yet it was not just the lack of religious knowledge and practice that amazed many Americans about Donald Trump. It was the almost complete lack of the character that is usually the fruit of sincere religion.

He was one of the most boastful men ever to run for the presidency, and this among a boastful tribe. He was preoccupied with crowd size. It became juvenile. When he spoke at Liberty University in 2016, his first words had to do with breaking an attendance record. He was in a church service at the time. He carried on an absurd Twitter war about the size of the crowd that attended his inauguration and did not let the matter drop for days. His behavior was typical of men who are unaffirmed as boys and who boast to compensate in later years. Yet there was so much in his life that should have offered a healing sense of accomplishment. None of it seemed to satisfy his soul.

For a man who claimed devotion to Christianity he had a distant relationship with the truth. He had learned the art of "truthful hyperbole" in his high-stakes real estate deals and brought this with him into the White House. In the first weeks of his presidency, huge portions of press conferences were devoted simply to whether he had told the truth in his public statements. News programs that once profiled interesting guests began focusing almost entirely upon fact-checking the president of the United States. The *Washington Post* printed daily charts to track the factual misstatements Trump made in office. Months into his presidency, the *Post* reported that not a day had gone by without a falsehood from the nation's chief executive.

He was also comfortable with violence. From the stage at a Kansas City rally, he mouthed to one offending protester, "I'll beat the crap out of you." Impatient over how long it took to remove protesters at a second rally, Trump told the crowd, "Part of the problem . . . is nobody wants to hurt each other anymore." When the audience took matters into their own hands at yet another campaign event, Trump cheered, "The audience hit back. That's what we need a little bit more of." In a famous episode, a white audience member punched a young black protestor already being removed from the arena. Trump's response was to offer to pay the white man's legal bills.

He was infuriating, offensive, and seemingly without restraint. He distorted facts, urged violence, spewed a mystifying brand of pride, and verbally pummeled anyone he opposed. He was so ignorant of his faith it was hard to believe he had ever been within view of a Bible, a church, a minister, or a religious truth he admired.

And yet.

There was another part of Donald Trump. It might not have been the largest part but it was there.

He became subdued and sometimes emotional when ministers gathered to pray for him. He seemed aware of sacred moments. He once called a religious advisor and said, "I know God says to forgive. But how do we know when to turn the other cheek and when to fight?"[12] This was a surprising question coming from a man who had touted the benefits of revenge his entire business career.

He was constantly given Bibles by fans and supporters, and though he could not use them all he had too much respect for "the good book" to throw the sacred volumes way. He had them stored in a room in Trump Tower.[13] He seemed genuinely eager to defend what he perceived to be religious liberty. He spoke so much about the Johnson Amendment and how he wanted to abolish it that even conservative clergy sometimes thought he went too far. Yet he believed it was an evil he could address. He knew he could not preach and was not much of an example of Christian character. He could, though, help to unchain God's servants and protect free speech.

He was a mixture, then: a maddening, unrepentant, ill-mannered, ever-bragging, ever-warring jumble of bad boy, billionaire, and aspiring saint. This is what we have as our forty-fifth president.

Yet he is not so secular or uncaring about religion as to leave it alone. He will target the Johnson Amendment. He will take counsel from religious conservatives. He will unapologetically try to protect the cause of Christians worldwide. He will, to the offense of millions of Americans, engineer a faith-based presidency on a vast scale.

Yet he will not be able to outstrip his ignorance and inexperience in matters of religion. He will sometimes speak of Muslims as though there are none in the US government. He will sometimes speak of Jews as though they are all diamond merchants eager for a deal. He will be suspicious of Mormons, doubtful of Roman Catholics, and unaware that Kurds, who are 97 percent Muslim, are among the best friends Middle Eastern Christians have.

He will be the most unusual president the United States has ever had. It is best we know his story and the forces that have shaped him. We are woven together with him now, in the fabric of American history.

PART 2

The Backstory

Had Donald Trump never become president of the United States, he would still be one of the most remarkable men of our times. His wealth is part of this, of course, as is his imprint upon entertainment, marketing, and the skyline of New York. Yet he is also remarkable as a sheer force of will. He has the determination and grizzled manner of one fleeing a life of suffering though he has known only luxury every day of his adult life. He is a brawler whose philosophy of life is captured in a single word: *victory*. He inherited this vision, enlarged it, and now carries it into the highest office his nation has to offer.

3 King

I was mostly interested in creating mischief, because for some reason I liked to stir things up, and I liked to test people.

Donald Trump[1]

The year was 1946. It was the first year in seventeen years in which the United States knew neither Great Depression nor World War. Harry Truman was in the White House. Frank Sinatra, Duke Ellington, the Andrews Sisters, and Bing Crosby provided the soundtrack, and *The Best Years of Our Lives* was the movie of the year.

War crimes trials were underway in Nuremburg and Tokyo. Winston Churchill gave his "Iron Curtain" speech in Fulton, Missouri, warning of a rising communist menace in Europe. President Truman ordered US troops to seize control of the nation's railroads when 250,000 railroad workers went on strike.

The United States owned ninety percent of the world's gold. The average house cost $5,600. The average annual wage was $2,500. If magazines from that time are any guide, men worked jobs or went to college on the GI Bill, smoked tobacco pipes, did a lot of bowling, and were constantly grilling meat in the backyard. Women came home from wartime factories, reveled in shiny, space-aged kitchens, led lives their mothers could barely have envisioned, and seemed to worry a great deal about what the neighbors thought.

AT&T announced the first car phone. Tupperware was new and would help to save the world. Bikinis went on sale in Paris. The Cannes Film Festival began in France.

At the University of Pennsylvania, the first programmable, general purpose electronic digital computer was introduced. It was called ENIAC, which stood for "Electronic Numerical Integrator and Computer." It cost $400,000 and filled a space thirty by fifty feet. Its first calculations were for construction of the hydrogen bomb.

It was the first full year of what came to be known as the "baby boom," which not only gave the nation more than seventy-six million babies over the following decade and a half but also gave the world a generation of firstborns—whether they had older siblings or not. The Great Depression slowed the pace of new births in the United States and World War II interrupted them. Marriage was also sidelined. When normality resumed in 1946, most new babies were either the first in their families or the first in their families for quite a while.

Common characteristics emerged in this first wave of the baby boom. These children were usually self-confident and assertive. They were, in the language of the day, a generation of "go-getters." They were also successful, usually from an early age. Their friends and siblings who were not firstborn wanted in on the fun and often acted as if they were firstborn too. This meant that, in 1946, American hospital delivery rooms were filled with the advance guard of an invading army that would revolutionize nearly everything about their nation and their world.

Donald Trump was among them. He was born on June 14 of this transitional year, the fourth child of Fred and Mary Trump, who lived on Wareham Street in Jamaica Estates, Queens, New York.

Much has been written about the stunning success of his later years. Much will be written about his even more stunning ascent to the White House. Yet the seeds of it all, particularly of his curious personality and religious views, were sown in childhood. The boy is always father to the man. This is especially the case in the life of Donald Trump. As he once said of himself, "I don't think people change very much. When I look at myself in the first grade and I look at myself now, I'm basically the same. The temperament is not that different."[2]

He was raised on family memories of a grandfather he never knew and on the steely resolve of a father who both molded and deformed him. Friedrich Trump, the grandfather, left Germany in 1885 at the age of sixteen to make a new life in America. He was avoiding military service in his native land. He was also dreaming of better things. His family's hopes rested upon him.

He joined his older sister, Katherine, and her husband in New York and began working as a barber. It was the trade he had trained for in Germany. He prospered enough over the next five years to move to the Great Northwest in 1891. True Americans always looked to the West for fortune. There, in Seattle, he owned and operated the Dairy Restaurant on 208 Washington Street. He succeeded in a variety of ventures in that city and then caught the gold fever that turned his gaze north to the Klondike.

In 1898, Friedrich moved to the rough, lakeside town of Bennett, British Columbia, and opened the New Arctic Restaurant and Hotel. He specialized in offering miners food, drink, and what one historian delicately referred to as "proximity to women."[3] Advertisements for the establishment promised "sporting ladies."[4]

He became a wealthy man and left the frozen north ahead of legal entanglements and declining gold prospects. In 1901, he returned to Germany to find a wife. He also hoped to live out his days in his native country. German law prevented it. Having seen so many youths escape the draft by fleeing to other countries, German officials adopted laws preventing these same men from resuming their lives in their homeland when they were too old to serve. Friedrich appealed vigorously and bitterly for four years. In 1905, resigned and dejected, he left for the United States with his pregnant wife, Elizabeth, at his side.

He returned to New York, again became a barber—this time a wealthy one—and invested in real estate. He had made it in America, he assured his son, Fred. It was a grand thing.

He died tragically, which added to the mystique that would long impress his grandson Donald. He was strolling with twelve-year-old Fred along Jamaica Avenue on the eve of Memorial Day, 1918. The two visited with friends and talked business with the realtors who had offices along that bustling boulevard. Suddenly, Friedrich turned to his son and said he felt sick. He returned home and went to bed. He was dead within hours. He was a casualty of the influenza epidemic that began sweeping the world in that year. Worldwide, five hundred million people were infected. As many as one hundred million died. In the United States, 28 percent of the population became infected and nearly 675,000 died.

Images from Friedrich's life would live vividly in Donald Trump's mind all his days. There was the scene of a sixteen-year-old German boy steaming into New York Harbor. There was the family memory of a young man who spoke no English making his way in the teeming city. A business in Seattle, a fortune won in the Klondike, cruel rejection by his homeland, and final, prosperous years in New York stirred young imaginations and formed themselves into a stubborn sense of destiny.

Fred Trump, Friedrich's son, lived out the mores of his father's life. Though he was only twelve when his father died, Fred partnered with his mother soon after to start a garage-building firm called Elizabeth Trump & Son. "I always wanted to be a builder," he admitted years later. "It was my dream as a boy, just as some kids want to be firemen."[5] He took classes at the local YMCA in carpentry and reading blueprints. Plumbing, masonry, and electrical wiring he learned from correspondence courses. His first job was building a garage for a neighbor. It was mediocre. He knew he had to improve. He apprenticed with successful builders, took courses at the Pratt Institute in Brooklyn, and built his first house when he was just two years out of high school. Since he was still under twenty-one, his mother had to sign the checks.

Barely two years later he had built nineteen homes in the Hollis neighborhood of Queens. He was ambitious and driven, determined to be the success he had dreamed. He built dozens of small, relatively affordable homes perfect for young couples and then branched out into higher-end homes modeled after Georgian mansions and English manor houses.

His business went stratospheric when he learned how to take advantage of new home financing regulations under Franklin Roosevelt's New Deal. Over the next half century, he built more than twenty-seven thousand low-income apartments and row houses, helped pioneer the concept of the supermarket, and was among the most prominent New York builders and philanthropists of his day.

He acquired an unfortunate reputation for skirting the ethical edge. In 1954 he was investigated by a US Senate committee for war profiteering. Nothing came of the charges, but the suspicions never fully lifted. The same occurred in 1973 when the Department of Justice filed a civil rights suit against The Trump Organization for violating the Fair Housing Act of 1968. The suit alleged that Trump refused to rent his apartments to black families. Decades before, he had been arrested during a Ku Klux Klan riot for failure to disperse. He may have been a mere bystander, but the arrest and the later civil rights charges against him moved many a New Yorker to think him a racist.

Folk singer Woody Guthrie, famous for his American classic "This Land Is Your Land," seemed to agree. He lived in one of

Trump's Brooklyn apartments in 1950. In a song he entitled "Old Man Trump," Guthrie painted a dark picture of Fred Trump as a slumlord who drew a "color line."

It is the imprint of such a man upon his famous son that will be of enduring interest to history. Fred was known as a relatively bloodless soul, a man devoted to his work and his family but little else. His children reported that he had no hobbies. He thought mainly about work and whatever new discipline was needed at home. When his sons got old enough to do manly things with their father, they found themselves traveling from construction site to construction site on Saturday and Sunday afternoons, forced to inspect progress and listen while foremen were chastised.

There is a memory of Fred recalled often by his children and his associates. Even on a hot New York day, he would arrive at a construction site wearing a tailored suit and stylish tie. He would walk the site, carefully examining every seam and surface. Workers and supervisors stood by nervously, preparing themselves for the predicted storm.

Inevitably, Fred would notice a nail on the ground, one that was not too scarred or bent. He would pick it up and put it in his pocket. Then he would see another. That one, too, ended up in his pocket. This might continue for hours. By the time he was done inspecting, the pockets of his expensive suit would be bulging with nails, all of which would be poured into the hands of a carpenter or a foreman accompanied by a rebuke for wastefulness. It was a scene repeated hundreds of times and it says much about the man. When Fred Trump died in 1999, he left his family an estate estimated at more than $300 million. To the end, he grew incensed when nails were wasted by his crews.

A story told by a grandson at Fred's funeral reveals something of his manner with the young. It seems that he frequently offered the young man a dollar bill. Each time he did, though, he described at length how hard he had worked for it and how much one dollar meant. The boy felt obligated to refuse every time. This apparently continued for years. Finally, the grandson chose to take the dollar. After he did, his grandfather never offered again. In the Fred Trump school of economics, lectures, guilt, and cold shoulders were the way to make a man.

Despite his often-demanding ways, Fred Trump was a shy man. He was awkward with people. He found them confusing. This made him appear distant, even uncaring. People who met him at receptions and parties often commented on the chilly experience it could be. It did not help that he was frequently tongue-tied. His children urged him to take a Dale Carnegie course in winning friends and influencing people. He did. It didn't help.

These traits made Fred Trump inaccessible to his children, his sons in particular. He was a demanding man without emotional depth, a perfectionist who expected excellence but who was incapable of rewarding with affection. Donald Trump said in later years that his father dispensed criticism freely but rarely gave out praise. It is not hard to imagine.

Fred was a stalwart believer in what he called the "racehorse theory." He was confident that there were superior people, thoroughbreds perhaps, who were innately gifted beyond average humans. When a superior man and woman mated, they produced a superior line. The Trumps were such a line, he believed, and so should naturally expect to rise above the unexceptional. Throughout his life, Donald would extol his "innate ability." Years later, his own son would tell reporters, "I'm a big believer in racehorse theory." Since his father was Donald Trump and his mother, Ivana Trump, made much of being a former Olympian, "I'd like to believe genetically I'm predisposed to better than average."[6]

This racehorse theory moved Fred to extol the value of competition. A favorite mantra was that he wanted his children to "Be killers." In fact, his two pet names for his son Donald were "King" and "Killer." He wanted his children to win. He thought failure was a result of defeatist thinking and laziness. He wouldn't have it. The words "You can do it if you try" were drilled into the souls of everyone he knew.

Everything was a competition. When he began to prosper, he graciously paid for his younger brother John's education. He sent him to Brooklyn Polytechnic Institute, to Columbia University for a master's degree, and then to the esteemed Massachusetts Institute of Technology, where John graduated with a PhD. These were expensive degrees and hard to earn. Fred's generosity and John's achievements ought to have bound the two brothers together. They ought to have basked in gratitude and joy. Instead, there was an edge. There was always an edge. It was fashioned on the anvil of competition. Speaking of his brother, Fred once turned to a friend and gloated, "He had the brains, but I made the money."[7]

Donald got the message. When he joined his father in business after college and then a few years later set out on his own, he made a revealing statement. The two men were gifted businessmen and might easily have formed a partnership that increased their wealth and graced their lives. Instead, Donald announced he would set his sights on Manhattan. He would leave Brooklyn and Queens to his father. Why? "It was good for me," he told reporters. "You know, being the son of somebody, it could have been competition to me. This way, I got Manhattan all to myself!"[8] These words were quoted in his father's *New York Times* obituary.

Fred's belief in industry came from his own father, Friedrich, and his belief in proper mental attitude came from his pastor of many years, Norman Vincent Peale. He accepted Peale's insistence that thoughts could change circumstances, that you could achieve it if you could conceive of it. The opposite was also true. A man failed because he believed he would. He became what he envisioned and strove for. God gave a person positive inner vision as a gift of grace. One had only to receive it and live it out. Doing so would lead to success. To refuse was sin and led to poverty of every kind. This was religion as Fred Trump passed it on to the next generation.

Such was the culture of the Trump home when Donald was born. This was the legacy handed down, one of industry and single-minded focus upon success. It valued achievement and sought victory as a measure of worth. Competitions won were nearly the meaning of life. This had its virtues. It produced wealth. It built reputations. It allowed for philanthropy. It propelled the next generation forward.

Donald Trump would also want us to know that his parents modeled a successful marriage for their children. In *The Art of the Deal*, he said, "I have a father who has always been a rock, very straight and very solid. . . . My mother is as much of a rock as my father. She is totally devoted to my father—that's what I grew up with."[9] This, too, was part of the Trump family culture and it obviously impressed Donald, whatever his own marriages seemed to reveal. Any marriage that lasts more than half a century is to be commended, and such an achievement was a centerpiece of the legacy Fred Trump left to his heirs.

Yet it was also a legacy that tortured. The father who demands but cannot affirm, who pushes but cannot praise, creates angry, boastful sons. Their anger masks the hurt of their rejection. Their boastfulness is their way of compensating for the lack of affirmation in earlier years. Couple this with a drive that transforms every human connection into a competition and it is likely that overachieving, aggressive, perhaps incomplete souls will emerge.

There is a description from Donald's early life that wrings a smile. It comes from the director of his elementary school. She remembered that "Donald was a beautiful little boy, very blond and buttery. He was a nice size for his age, very attractive, social and outgoing. He wasn't fat, but he was sturdy, and really quite jolly."[10] It is pleasant to think of the child Donald Trump as "jolly." It is the word "buttery" that friends will not let him forget.

We can envision him playing in front of the two-story Tudor revival house his father owned. It was conveniently located a few blocks from the Grand Central Parkway, a lifeline to the city of New York. Two years after Donald was born, when his younger brother Robert was still on the way, Fred Trump bought two lots that adjoined the property and built a twenty-three-room mansion on Midland Parkway. Its colonial style portico, stained-glass crest, and six huge white columns were the talk of the neighborhood.

This house was not only the backdrop of Donald's early life but also part of what set him and his family apart. He was a Trump. That name already carried import and heft. This was confirmed by the chauffeur-driven limousine his father took to work and by the staff that tended the house—if the dozens of signs all over Queens and Brooklyn advertising Trump buildings were not evidence enough. Donald Trump was born into a family empire on the rise. He absorbed this reality and, in time, made it his own. It is one of the defining realities of his life.

Even the Trump children's memories of their mother were largely tied to public impressions. Donald recalled in *The Art of the Deal* that his mother "always had a flair for the dramatic and the grand," that she loved "splendor and magnificence."[11] His sister reported that their mother was a woman who reveled in attention: "When the lights went up, she was the star."[12] A common family theme emerges in these memories too. "My mother was silently competitive," Donald recalled in later years. "She was a very competitive person but you wouldn't know that. She had a great fighting spirit, like Braveheart."[13] Always competitiveness is the measure. Always the gaze of others is in view.

The Trump children seldom reference lessons of character and faith learned from their mother. They must have occurred. She once assured a clergyman that she had worked to embed the benefits of religion in her children. "I tried to get it into their heads that they had to believe," she said. "Whether it shows or not, it's in there because I put it in there."[14] Such was the steel and determination of this woman.

Yet whatever lessons of faith his mother may have taught, they do not seem to have gone far in shaping young Donald Trump's life. It is true that he was gifted. It is true that he did well in school when he chose to, excelled in sports, and was a natural leader among his peers—all when he chose to. Yet most recollections of young Donald are not of a gifted, cooperative boy but rather of a difficult, rebellious, even dangerous child. More than a few adult witnesses to his early years use the word *terror*.

In fact, it is hard to connect the image of Donald as "beautiful," "outgoing," and "jolly" as reported by his elementary school director with the descriptions of him we have from shortly thereafter. His late elementary school years are marked by anger, even violence. He seems frustrated and to a degree that drives him to extremes.

He once became so frustrated with a teacher that he hit the man in the face. He had concluded that the teacher did not know his field and so he gave him a black eye. He was only in the second grade at the time. The Donald Trump of later years considered this "assertive." In fact, this later version of the man sees virtue in the boyhood version of himself hitting the teacher. "I'm not proud of that, but it's clear evidence that even early on I had a tendency to stand up and make my opinions known in a very forceful way."[15]

Yet more was occurring than just an opinionated boy demanding to be heard. It is obvious that something was wrong. He threw erasers at school and food at birthday parties. He argued with everyone and had special ire for anyone who dared approach him with authority. One elementary school teacher reported that Donald "would sit with his arms folded, with this look on his face—I would use the word surly—almost daring you to say one thing or another that wouldn't settle with him."[16] Another insisted, "He was a pain. There are certain kids that need attention all the time. He was one of those."[17] When the family went to camps in upstate New York for the summer,

Donald was always "an ornery kid, the kind that tried to get out of activities whenever he could."[18]

There is a story Donald tells from these early years. He was playing with his blocks and building an ambitious structure. To complete his vision, he borrowed his younger brother Robert's blocks as well. When he was finished with the project, he was so pleased with what he had created that he glued all the blocks together. He wanted his edifice to endure. "And that was the end of Robert's blocks," Donald reported years later with glee.[19]

He liked, as he often said in later years, to push people, to create tension, to see how far he could assert himself to the misery of others. He saw this not as malicious but rather, in one of his favorite terms of explanation, as aggressive. This word is usually paired with *assertive*. In Trump's mind, these terms cover a multitude of sins. They are the excuse for misbehavior, the rationale even for violent acts. Somewhere during his early life, he had come to believe that to push back, to hit hard, to demand to be heard were virtues. They were not only acceptable, they led to power. They made him exceptional.

He must have learned this from someone, seen it modeled and portrayed. He must have known aggression was prized by someone he respected. In an interview given years later, he explained. The subject was how he won respect from his father. The answer was simple. While others in Fred Trump's life retreated, "I used to fight back all the time."[20]

It became his ethos, his code. Some boys are unruly and even violent because they are in pain, because they are unhappy and angry with the world. Donald Trump saw fighting back as a tactic. It was how he kept people at bay. It was how he conquered the challenges of his life. It was how he won what he perceived as respect. Fight back. Hit hard. Apologize for nothing. Always be ready for another round.

Though Fred liked seeing the steel in his son's soul, he realized soon after Donald turned thirteen that he could no longer rule him. Teachers complained. Pastors complained. There was constant fighting at home. Adding to it all, Fred discovered that his son was regularly sneaking into Manhattan on the subway. He learned of this when he found a collection of knives and switchblades Donald had amassed. It was the era of *West Side Story* and switchblades were cool. Donald liked the way they felt in his hand. He liked the sense of power and threat they gave him. Fred might have found a way to overlook the disobedience of his son in going to Manhattan but stockpiling weapons was simply too much. He had to do something. "That was the incident," a friend said, "that turned Donald's father into thinking he should go away to school."[21]

It was one of those fortuitous parental decisions upon which destinies turn. The year was 1959. Donald was in behavioral freefall. Fred may not have known exactly what caused the storms in his son's soul but he did know when something had moved beyond his control. And Donald had.

The solution was to enroll him in military school and the best choice was New York Military Academy. It was situated fifty miles north of New York City, not far from the United States Military Academy at West Point. Since 1889, it had been the kind of place where concerned parents enrolled their unruly sons. The words above the school's main entrance captured the hopes of generations: "Courageous and Gallant Men Have Passed Through These Portals." Fred Trump may have been more impressed with the school's slogan: "Set Apart for Excellence." The words and the promise they made had impressed mobster John Gotti and Cuban president Fulgencio Batista enough to send their sons to the school.

It was a bullying place that made quick work of bullies. The 450 cadets in Trump's era rose early each morning to the sound of a bugle and quickly dressed in the standard gray shirt and pants and maroon tie. No civilian clothes were worn. Days were filled with classes, chapels, and military drills. Inspections were frequent and dealt with everything a cadet wore, owned, or lived in—gloves, hat bands, cartridge belts, shoes, sinks, toilets, brass buttons, sheets, and breastplates.

The first months at the school were hell. Tears were common, as were pleas to call home or leave. Plebes learned to dress, salute, march, and do anything an upperclassman required, from push-ups to reciting obscure sections of the school handbook. Drinking, gambling, stealing, hitchhiking, possession of pornography, and even "not walking properly" could result in demerits or dismissal. Hazing played a role too. Trump may have been required to do what upperclassmen required of other cadets—kiss the school's mascot, a donkey, "on the ass."

He found himself in a system intended to humiliate, control, and remake. Seemingly angry people barked at him to keep his mouth closed, keep in step, and do every task of the day in the prescribed manner—from taking a shower to doing his homework, from getting to classes on time to writing his mother. Nothing escaped scrutiny, nothing went unremarked upon. Every experience was a laboratory for testing mettle and building character.

New York Military Academy made Donald Trump into an exceptional man. It gave him confidence that was earned rather than stolen. It helped him channel his aggression and taught him self-mastery. It broke him down to show him how pitiful he was and then rebuilt him into a skilled and competent man. He would always be Fred Trump's son, but he would never lose the snap and the shine of the NYMA cadet.

He also came under the influence of a surrogate father who was profoundly shaping many young male lives at the time. Hugh Hefner's *Playboy* magazine had launched in 1953, and by the time of Trump's academy years it was one of the most talked about publications in the nation. Though pornography was forbidden at the school, copies of the magazine found their way into the barracks and were much discussed by the cadets. The "Playboy Philosophy" evoked images of sophisticated, worldly wise young men finding fulfillment in achievement, in the material trappings of wealth, and by casting off outworn moral restraints. Pleasures awaited such men, and most of the cadets at NYMA wanted to be among them, no one more than Donald Trump.

Yet a seriousness of purpose was also embedded in Trump's life during these years. Much of this was the doing of Colonel Theodore Dobias. He was the screaming, battle-hardened mentor Donald Trump needed. Dobias had joined the Marines at the age of seventeen and fought during World War II with the storied Tenth Mountain Division. He watched a thousand of his comrades die on the Italian Peninsula, where he also viewed the mutilated body of dictator Benito Mussolini hanging from the awning of a gas station in Milan. He returned to NYMA, finished his education, and began his career as a teacher and coach.

Dobias remembered all his life his first glimpse of Trump. Surprisingly, what impressed him most was that the boy was so coachable. In the press of NYMA, young Trump had become eager to please, even teachable. Dobias, a maker of men, saw that Cadet Trump could be shaped in ways other cadets could not.

Cadet Trump did well in the classroom, but it was on the athletic field that his character was shaped. Dobias's coaching philosophy was straight from the playbook of famed Green Bay Packers coach Vince Lombardi: "I coached baseball and football, and I taught them that winning wasn't everything, it was the only thing."[22] Young Trump did not have to be convinced of this approach to sports, or to life as a whole. He had learned it from his father and from his own often-inflated sense of self-importance and destiny. He easily picked up on the Lombardi/Dobias approach and made it his own. As Dobias remembered, Trump would "tell his teammates, 'We're out here for a purpose. To win.' He always had to be number one, in everything. He was a conniver even then. A real pain in the a—. He would do anything to win."[23]

Donald attended New York Military Academy at a time when coaches could strike cadets to make their meaning known. Dobias hit him often. He also worked him. He saw the potential and wanted to see it fulfilled, but he also knew that the arrogance and surliness might get in the way. Dobias yelled, humiliated, made Trump do push-ups and run laps as punishment, and tried to show the boy the extent of his gifts.

The World War II vet could be fatherly too. He checked often to make sure Donald's grades were good. He urged him to think of his impact on other cadets. He spoke the words he thought would ignite character and passion in Trump's soul. He must have eventually seen what he was looking for. Not only did Trump become a stellar athlete and leader but Dobias also made him an unofficial baseball coach. It was a great honor, particularly since it came from the toughest, most revered warrior at the school.

Dobias also understood what Trump endured at home. He had met Fred Trump and watched the man's manner with his son. It saddened him. With wisdom that came from years of watching cadets with their parents, he understood of the Trumps what others perhaps could not see. "The father was really tough on the kid," Dobias recounted. "He was very German. He came up on a lot of Sundays and would take the boy out to dinner. Not many did that. But he was very tough."[24]

It is revealing that years later Trump did not recall his relationship with Dobias in tender terms. He did not speak of Dobias as a father figure, as a man who invested in him and helped to make him much of what he became. Instead, he recalls mainly that he learned how to manipulate Dobias to get what he wanted.

As he explained in *The Art of the Deal*, Trump was immediately wary of Dobias. "Very quickly I realized that I wasn't going to make it with this guy by trying to take him on physically. A few less fortunate kids chose that route, and they ended up getting stomped."[25]

Instead Trump describes how he bested Dobias through intelligence. In fact, this is nearly the entire reason that Dobias appears in *The Art of the Deal* at all. He explains that he used his "head to get around the guy. I figured out what it would take to get Dobias on my side. In a way, I finessed him. It helped that I was a good athlete, since he was the baseball coach and I was the captain of the team. But I also learned how to play *him*."[26]

It is perhaps not surprising that, in a book on winning through deal making, Trump would describe his relationship with his college mentor as a competition. It is natural, in this light, that he reports that he bested his opponent. Accomplished men often have mentors in early life. Usually, they speak of them with affection and gratitude. They laud the investment made, the great good done in their lives through a single, devoted individual. It would be nice to hear such sentiments from Trump. Yet referring to Dobias as a capable opponent was the best Trump could do. Always there is a competition. Always there is a test of wits. Nearly always, in his retelling, Donald Trump wins.

In fairness, he had discovered himself at NYMA. He was stepping into his own. His was a school in which a cadet measured himself against others nearly every minute of the day. A man rose or fell on the strength of his gifts and how those gifts were appraised by others. Trump fared well, very well, in this environment, and it is perhaps part of what makes him frame all his academy memories in terms of competition.

Some of his fellow cadets remembered him in kinder terms. One friend recalled, "You could always go to Donald and he would figure out how to get things done."[27] Another experienced a new gentle authority in Trump's life. "I came back from a trip to New York once, and I was five minutes late, and he just looked at me. He never yelled at anyone. He would just look at you, the eyebrows kind of raised. The kind of look that said you can't disappoint him."[28] More than a few who knew Trump at the time noted the sense of destiny that attended him. "He was self-confident and very soft-spoken, believe it or not, as if he knew he was just passing time until he went on to something greater."[29]

It was this matter of destiny, of a call to greatness, that was often on Trump's mind during his NYMA years. He assured his roommates regularly that he would be famous one day. He wanted to be the best. He dreamed of it, and announced it to his friends as though it was a certain fate. New York Military Academy gave him the confidence, the skill, and the record of achievement that seemed to confirm his ambitions.

He graduated in May 1964. He would turn eighteen the next month. He would attend two universities while working for his father and it would all propel him into the decades of real estate and entertainment success that in turn propelled him to the presidency. He would take his gifts and his demons with him into it all.

There is a sad recollection from a student who knew Trump during his Academy days. It reveals that a Trump family obsession stayed with Donald during his NYMA years and exacted a price. The words describe well the curse of competition that would follow him all his life.

> People liked him, but he didn't bond with anyone. I think it was because he was too competitive and with a friend you don't always compete. It was like he had this defensive wall around him, and he wouldn't let anyone get close. He didn't distrust everybody, but he didn't trust them, either.[30]

4 | Killer

> When you are in business you need to get even with people
> who screw you. You need to screw them back fifteen times
> harder . . . go for the jugular, attack them in spades!
>
> Donald Trump[1]

The human soul seems to emit a magnetic pull. It draws to itself that which confirms what is already believed. It seems to amass evidence for the case it is making against the world. Some would say that this is little more than a person's soul distorting reality to accommodate the deformities of his or her life. It may be true. The danger, of course, is that people live out the lessons they think life is teaching when those lessons may in fact be merely the projections of their own souls.

There is an experience in the early adult life of Donald Trump that seems to confirm this. In November 1964, he had the opportunity of attending the opening ceremonies for the Verrazano-Narrows Bridge in New York. Since this was the longest and highest suspension bridge in the world, it was much celebrated. The opening ceremonies drew massive crowds, with certain elegant receptions and parties open only to the elite. Fred Trump's reputation allowed

Donald to attend whatever he wished, and so the day should have been a happy memory for both father and son.

For the younger Trump, though, the affair was occasion for confirming a bitter truth of life. As he looked over the glorious vista of the ceremony, his eyes fell upon Othmar Hermann Ammann. He knew something of this man's story. Ammann was one of the greatest bridge builders in the world. The Swiss-born genius had built or designed the George Washington Bridge, the Bayonne Bridge, the Triborough Bridge, the Box-Whitestone Bridge, the Walt Whitman Bridge, and the Throgs Neck Bridge. He had even assisted in construction of the Golden Gate Bridge in San Francisco.

Now, though, during the Verrazano-Narrows ceremony, the eminent builder sat alone, largely ignored. Few knew who he was and fewer cared. One who did know the man was Donald Trump. The fact that Ammann would be dead the next year may have played into the memory of this moment in Trump's mind, and thus helped to shape a hard-edged conclusion about human nature. "I realized then and there," he later recalled, "that if you let people treat you how they want, you'll be made a fool. I realized then and there something I would never forget: I don't want to be made anybody's sucker."[2]

If he was telling the truth about forming this impression the moment he saw Othmar Ammann that day at the Verrazano Bridge, then the lesson he drew seems alien to his experience. He was only eighteen and he was certainly no one's "sucker." Nor was there any threat he might be. He was a son of privilege who had known only private schools, an elite military academy education, and the home of a multimillionaire. He had seldom been mistreated and was rarely made a fool. In fact, he had known few genuine hardships. It is true he was required to have a paper route. His father wanted him to know the value of a dollar. Yet when it rained, Fred Trump allowed Donald to deliver his papers from the comfort of the family's chauffeur-driven limousine. The boy was hardly being abused.

Still, the memory of that day in 1964 poured its meaning into his cynical, contentious view of the world. Trump came to believe and often said that a man could accomplish much, make his contribution, benefit millions, and still be ignored. In fact, he could be left lonely and neglected on the sidelines of history. It happened because he became someone's "sucker." He got played. He got out-maneuvered. His deal was bad. A man had to ever be on his guard. They would use you if they could. Then you would die, lonely and ignored. It was a fate to be feared and avoided at all costs.

This, then, was the brazen, caustic, punishing attitude Donald Trump carried into the next decades of his life. He attended Fordham for two years, commuting from his parents' home and working for his father. He then transferred to the University of Pennsylvania, largely because the prestigious Wharton School of Finance was there and because U-Penn was one of the few schools in the nation that offered an undergraduate business degree in real estate. Trump knew what he wanted to do and saw no reason to major in any subject except the one essential to his dreams.

He learned largely that he had little to learn. He would say often in later years that the main thing he learned at Wharton was not to be impressed with academic degrees. He felt he knew more than his professors and far more than his fellow students. He found nothing exceptional about his teachers or his classmates and this fed a sense of superiority that has emanated from all his life.

The truth is that he had already received a stellar education from his father. His academic major was, essentially, the life of Fred Trump. There was little he didn't know about real estate apart from the abstract theory his professors emphasized. He had walked construction sites year after year. He had sat at his father's side and learned to analyze markets and evaluate investments. He had also overheard negotiations with bankers, the wooing of investors, and the coaxing of laborers. He had watched his father choose sinks, test flooring, and pick up usable nails by the thousands. He remembered all he had learned. The truth was Donald knew the field almost as well as his professors.

Classmates later recalled that when Trump spoke to his professors during class it was like one insider speaking to another. They looked on amazed. Trump's experience had prepared him well. It was why he was able to report that the main thing he received from Wharton was a Wharton degree—not knowledge, just the degree: "In my opinion, that degree doesn't prove very much, but a lot of people I do business with take it very seriously and it's considered very prestigious. So all things considered, I'm glad I went to Wharton."[3]

Upon graduation, he went to work full-time for his father and lived at home with his parents. He already knew that he did not want to spend his life doing his father's brand of real estate. As he told his roommates at NYMA, he would use his father as a model, but he intended to go further. Fred Trump's world was rent-controlled and government-monitored and far too much work for the yield. Donald dreamed of a more elegant life, someplace far removed.

He needed a foothold from which to launch, though, and Elizabeth Trump & Son was his best bet. It was successful. It was run by family. He could rise quickly. It bore the Trump name that he planned to parlay into even greater riches and fame.

He cut his teeth with a project in Cincinnati, Ohio. He and his father reopened a 1,200-unit apartment complex called Swifton Village. They purchased the largely defunct facility for just under $6 million, invested $100,000, and rebranded the project as something shiny and new. There were challenges. The apartments were lower-end and drew tenants who threw their trash out of the window and might easily answer the door with a gun when late rent was being collected. Needing a better class of tenants, the Trumps put nearly a million dollars more into the project and made sure to upgrade appearances to meet more elevated tastes.

They focused on cosmetic changes that appealed to the middle-class tenants they sought. They installed white shutters and "beautiful colonial white doors." They painted hallways, sanded and refinished floors, and landscaped the grounds. Then they advertised. It had seldom been done before for an apartment complex of this type, but it gave the Trumps a chance to elevate their brand in the eyes of the public. Soon, they reached 100 percent occupancy.

Eventually, they were taking in $700,000 a year. It was time to sell. They found an interested buyer in Prudent Real Estate Investment Trust and negotiated a sale for $12 million. They had profited $6 million from their investment.

It was the first major real estate project of Donald Trump's life, and it contained all the elements that would become so familiar throughout his career. He bought an overlooked property while critics scoffed. He invested in a massive upgrade. He majored on cosmetic changes—what New York real estate wags called "curb appeal" or the "wow factor." He worked to draw a better class of tenants. He devoted himself to the art of brand management and to an aggressive style of promotion. He sold at the right time and made a huge profit. It was the manner of a lifetime. The size and glitz of the projects would increase; the personality behind it would will himself to global celebrity. Always, there were the almost intentional controversies, the huge amounts of bluff, and the unapologetic self-promotions.

Soon after this first victory he began hitting his stride. He was appointed president of the family firm and quickly changed its name to The Trump Organization. Then began the string of investments and developments that launched his storied career. He set his sights on Manhattan as he said he would and struck out on his own. His father helped him but seemed to understand his son's need to soar above the rest.

In 1978, Trump remodeled the Grand Hyatt Hotel, previously the historic Commodore Hotel, located right next to Grand Central Terminal. He also negotiated for the construction of Trump Tower, the fifty-eight-story skyscraper in Midtown Manhattan that would become his home, The Trump Organization's headquarters, and the crown jewel of the Trump empire and brand. It was completed in 1983 and celebrated for its role in helping New York City recover from tormented years of decline.

He branded himself as a real estate genius and almost dared competitors and the press to disagree. They couldn't. He produced too much evidence. There was the time in 1986, for example, that he took over construction of the Wollman Rink in Central Park and completed it in three months, well under budget. Then, in a classic Trump move, he offered to operate the rink for one year with profits going to charity in exchange for the rink's concession rights.

In 1985, he bought Mar-a-Lago, the historic Palm Beach, Florida, home built by Marjorie Merriweather Post, and has used it since as a southern retreat. Not surprisingly, he has also turned it into a private club with annual dues ranging above $250,000 a year.

He had long been intrigued by the profitability of casinos and in 1984 opened Harrah's at Trump Plaza. Then, in 1988, he acquired the Taj Mahal in Atlantic City. These ventures were sometimes ill-fated but, predictably, Trump emerged unscathed when he negotiated for restructuring debt in his favor and carefully managed public perceptions at every step.

He built his reputation on high-dollar, high-profile real estate deals but his greatest strengths were those he used in making himself a global brand. He was hard to avoid. He adorned magazine covers, appeared on every television talk show of note, and managed to keep himself constantly in the news. He seemed to live by the maxim that all PR is good PR, that it doesn't matter what they say about you so long as they spell your name right.

He licensed his name and image and began making huge sums for offering both to flashy projects. He bought and sold sports franchises, beauty pageants, and modeling agencies. He lent his talents to board games, wineries, and a brand of steaks. He took over airlines and founded lines of clothing. He wrote bestselling books like *The Art of the Deal* and often signed them with the word "Win!" next to his name. It had become the meaning of his life.

Nobody doubted he was Fred Trump's son. Donald had become both "King" and "Killer," just as his father had hoped. He was certainly no one's "sucker" now.

Behind the scenes, though, he experienced a loss that both wounded and hardened him. On his military academy dresser he had always kept a picture of a good-looking blond man standing next to an airplane. It was Freddy Jr., Donald's older brother. Almost everything the world needed to know about this man was registered in his handsome, friendly face. He was funny. He was playful. He could light up a room. He thought his own thoughts. He was eager to please. Donald loved him completely.

Freddy Jr. was six years older than his younger brother and was supposed to be the heir apparent. He was supposed to become his father's clone and be a real estate superstar celebrated the world over. This was the dream he was born into, and this was the expectation he felt from his parents nearly every day of his life.

Nature worked against him. He was neither as smart nor as athletic as his brothers and sisters. Instead, he spent hours lost in thought. He was a skinny, nervous boy who fidgeted and jerked in just the way that would infuriate a focused, demanding, image-conscious father like Fred Sr. Though the elder Trump would not have said it out loud, Fred Jr. was a disappointment.

The truth is that he was a gifted man made for a different life than his family envisioned. He did not go to Kew Forest School, the elite establishment his siblings attended. He instead attended St. Paul's, an Episcopal boys' prep school on Long Island. This worried his father. As one friend from the time remembered, "I think Freddy's father feared that he would be an aesthete fairy, a little English gentleman. It was almost as though he thought prep school was emasculating his son, that he was having the aggressive instincts schooled out of him and he was being turned into an Ivy League wimp."[4]

Still, against type, Fred Jr. tried to fulfill his father's hopes. He applied to the esteemed Wharton School of Finance but failed to get in. He went instead to Lehigh University in central Pennsylvania. He enrolled in the Air Force ROTC and, oddly, said he was Jewish to win acceptance into a Jewish fraternity. He was desperate to belong.

When he graduated in 1958, he became his father's assistant. It was an arrangement doomed to fail and certain to wound. Fred Sr. wanted a killer. Fred Jr. was competent and friendly but lacked his father's gifts for saving pennies and bullying people.

Those outside the family saw the flaws in this arrangement before the father and son did. Friends understood that Fred Jr. was playing a role, was trying to be the tough man of business his father demanded. This only set the son up for failure and exposed him to his father's abuse. Fred Sr. thought nothing of viciously chastising his son in front of others for any offense. When his daughter asked why he never praised Fred Jr. for the good things he did, Fred Sr. replied, "Why? He's supposed to do a good job." The value of praise was lost on the man.

Fred Jr. endured these tortures as long as he could. Eventually, he left the family business to fulfill his dream of becoming an airline pilot. He married a flight attendant, had two children, and enjoyed flying for TWA until his drinking bested him. He spent his later years in the alcoholic's downward spiral. He died on September 26, 1981, at the age of forty-three.

Guilt and grief took their toll. Donald understood that Fred Jr. "had perhaps the hardest time in our family."[5] He also adored his older brother in the tender way that younger brothers often do. "Handsome as could be, he loved parties and had a great, warm personality and a real zest for life. He didn't have an enemy in the world."[6] His older brother's death was for Donald, "the saddest part in what I've been through."[7]

He also seemed to realize that it was his family's sometimes toxic culture that brought Fred Jr. to his end. "Our family environment, the competitiveness, was a negative for Fred," Donald told *Playboy* magazine in 1990.[8] He perhaps did not realize this early enough. When Fred Jr. first left the Trump firm to become a pilot, Donald compared this new profession to driving a bus. "Come on, Freddy," he had said. "What are you doing? You're wasting your time."[9] Writing years later in *The Art of the Deal*, Trump notes solemnly, "I regret now that I ever said that."[10]

Yet in the same way that he drew hard-edged lessons from seeing Othmar Ammann sitting alone at the dedication of the Verrazano-Narrows Bridge in 1984, Donald wrung bitter certainties from the death of his brother. Fred Jr's problem, he concluded, was that he "just wasn't a killer."[11] This was his "fatal mistake." The overriding truth of the whole experience was that "man is the most vicious of all animals, and life is a series of battles ending in victory or defeat. You just can't let people make a sucker out of you."[12] Years later, he spoke of his brother's death as though explaining his life philosophy: "I saw people really taking advantage of Fred and the lesson I learned was always to keep up my guard one hundred percent."[13]

These would seem lessons suggested more by the bent of Trump's soul than by the tragic death of his brother. Still, they were lessons that would haunt his soul and help to make him the bludgeoning figure he became on the American business and entertainment scenes.

It is as difficult to explain as his angry, violent ways in boyhood. Throughout his life, he unashamedly spoke in terms one might more naturally expect of an abused child, a member of an oppressed minority group, or a refugee from a ravaged war zone. "Life is about survival," he often pontificated. "It's always about survival."[14] He spoke as a man familiar only with the dark side of human nature: "I think I probably expect the worst of people because I've seen too much. But I think it's a very nice trait to have."[15] This was odd. He had seldom known anything but opulence and ease.

He had the manner of a street fighter, the *blitzkrieg* approach to business more common to a German tank commander during World War II. People marveled that one reared in comfort and luxury could unashamedly speak as though he had been deprived, could conduct himself with the vengeance and viciousness of a man denied his rights all his days.

Where had it all come from? It was, without doubt, the imprint of Fred Trump upon his soul. His father had wanted a Killer King. He got one, a son as tough, focused, seemingly soulless, and as committed to business as total war as the father had ever been. Yet it seems, too, that it came from somewhere deep within Donald himself. He had been harsh and bombastic since childhood. Teachers called him "maladjusted." The less understanding called him "a terror."

Whatever he was, there was an anger, a jut-jawed resentment that had radiated from him almost since birth. New York Military Academy taught him to manage it but could not extract it from his life. Another man—his brother, Fred Jr., for example—might have conducted business as a means to a happy life of abundance and generosity. Yet another might have entered commerce for its beauty and its comradery. Donald Trump did it to win. This, to him, was the meaning of life. Any other vision belonged to "suckers."

He found an ally in this approach to life and business in grizzled warrior Roy Cohn. The two met at an opportune moment. On October 15, 1973, the US Justice Department had filed suit against The Trump Organization charging racial prejudice in its renting practices. Black renters in particular, the suit insisted, were either turned away or charged exorbitant rates. The suit infuriated Trump both because there were more than a few happy black tenants in his apartments and because the feds had leveled the same kind of charges against The Trump Organization before.

He met Roy Cohn shortly thereafter. He already knew him by reputation. Cohn was one of twentieth-century America's most unusual personalities. He became famous in the 1950s when he worked with Senator Joseph McCarthy in unearthing communists in the US government and in Hollywood. Cohn survived both the declining popularity of this cause and the early death of its champion—McCarthy died at forty-eight of alcohol-related liver disease—to become a renowned fixer, influence peddler, and courtroom brawler.

Cohn's life was defined by contradictions. He was Jewish but also an outspoken racist and anti-Semite. He was gay but frequently launched into angry rants about the evils of homosexuality. He was a sentimental patriot and yet at home in New York's criminal underworld. He could be vicious to enemies but tender to his friends. He lived by an exacting personal code of conduct that was far from any ethical code average Americans or US courts could understand. He was also an eccentric. Some wondered if he was sane. He once put a pen in the hand of a dead man to amend a will.

Trump met Cohn when the two men were seated at tables near each other at Le Club in New York. As Trump remembered the meeting in *The Art of the Deal*, he immediately began taking jabs at the famous tough-guy attorney. The reason? "I like to test people."

It was becoming standard Trump procedure. Pick a fight. Test the mettle. Make an ally or walk away. With Cohn, he went for what he thought was the jugular. "I don't like lawyers. I think all they do is delay deals, instead of making deals, and every answer they give you is no, and they are always looking to settle instead of a fight."[16]

Cohn surprised Trump by saying he agreed. We can almost visualize the sly smile that must have crossed Trump's face. He pressed further. "I'm just not built that way. I'd rather fight than fold, because as soon as you fold once, you get the reputation of being a folder."[17] Cohn was a man easily bored and short on patience. "Is this just an academic conversation?" he asked.

Trump welcomed the opportunity to leave the abstract. He explained that the conversation was not academic, that in fact the government had just filed a civil rights suit against his firm alleging that blacks had been discriminated against in Trump housing projects. He explained that his own lawyers had recommended that The Trump Organization settle. Trump despised such counsel and was eager for a fight.

"What do you think I should do?" he finally asked. Cohn answered as anyone who knew him might expect: "My view is tell them to go to hell."[18] The veteran courtroom brawler then explained that Trump should fight the charges in court and force the government to prove discrimination, which Cohn thought would be a hard thing to do given that there were black families in Trump's buildings.

It was the counsel Trump had hoped for. Cohn was his kind of fighter—a brutal, "baseball bat to the knees" kind of attorney who shared Trump's belief in hitting first, hitting hardest, and hitting until the other side surrendered. He hired Cohn on the spot.

What won Trump was not just Cohn's "total war" approach to practicing law but also his loyalty. Though he was not yet thirty at the time, Trump had already acquired disdain for the kind of men who made careers of promising integrity but seldom remained true to a friend or client. He despised the backstabbers. He had nothing but spite for those devoted only to themselves, those who would betray a friend at the first opportunity. Cohn was different, Trump believed. "You could count on him. . . . He was never two-faced. . . . Roy was the sort of guy who'd be there at your hospital bed, long after everyone else had bailed out, literally standing by you to the death."[19] In short, Cohn was a "total genius," but the kind who would "kill for somebody that he liked."[20]

The case was handled in vintage Cohn style. On January 12, 1974, Cohn and Trump held a press conference at the New York Hilton to announce they were suing the federal government for $100 million in damages. The civil rights claims were "irresponsible and baseless."

Investigators failed to produce a single person who had suffered discrimination by The Trump Organization, Cohn claimed.

Federal attorneys were stunned. They had never faced such a vicious, public counterpunch to a civil rights suit. Rather than the high-profile, easily won case they had hoped for, the government attorneys ended up agreeing to a minor settlement that The Trump Organization naturally spun as a victory.

Cohn not only became Trump's attorney and the public face of The Trump Organization but also became a mentor. He was savage, merciless, and seemingly fearless. Trump loved him. He kept a particularly evil looking photo of Cohn in his desk drawer. During a meeting, if things were not going his way, he'd pull the photo out and say, "This is my lawyer. If you don't straighten up, you'll be dealing with him." This reassured his partners and terrified anyone who dared cross him. The two men forged a steely bond tempered by rage, vengeance, and devotion to victory at nearly any cost. This spirit would shape Trump's business career and help fuel his rise to the White House.

The question is, why? It was easy to understand the fierce, vindictive, bitter ways of Roy Cohn. He was gay in a heterosexual world, Jewish in a largely Christian America. He was also odd-looking, his bulging eyes and flashy style making him a laughingstock nationwide. He had tethered himself to one of the most despised politicians in American history and become a despised figure himself. It was no surprise that he made gladiator spectacles of courtrooms and cynically brokered power among the powerful. It was all born of a lust for vengeance and vindication. This was the life of Roy Cohn.

It was not as easy to understand the raging ways of Donald Trump. What had sunk its teeth into his soul? What tortured him in the night, this son of wealth and status? What justified his fuming use of business as war by other means? What made him the narcissistic, vengeful, punishing creature he was during his years of storied success?

The answer can only be found in a conspiracy of influences. Certainly, his father made him see the world as a place filled with those who would take advantage. You had to be the best. You had to dominate. It was why Fred Trump called his son "King" and "Killer." He was making of his son what his snarling view of the world demanded.

He was also taught at New York Military Academy that winning was the meaning of life. Cadets went to chapel each week to present themselves before a God who could help them achieve excellence if he chose. They worshiped him. They implored his help. Theirs, though, was the law of the jungle—competition as the means of natural selection, as the mechanism for determining survival of the fittest. Donald Trump thrived in that environment. He truly was both "King" and "Killer." Yet he was so excessively committed to competition as the meaning of life that he drove friends away and found himself largely alone. He stepped into the world as an adult, then, believing he existed to conquer and acquire.

Always there was the factor of Donald Trump's innate nature. He seemed to have come from the womb at war with the world. He was the evidently troubled boy who sat in elementary school classrooms resistant as a statue, defying his teachers to do their worst. He is the one who thought nothing of punching a music teacher in the face for not knowing enough—and this in the second grade. His hard-bitten father knew that his son was more hard-bitten still and sent him off to military school before he destroyed himself. He learned to manage but could not conquer the anger in his soul.

His rise in business, then, was informed by a cynical view of humankind. This is odd given that capitalism is rooted in the belief that human beings need each other, that their diversity of gifts is what powers advancement, and that cooperation and harmony are essential to prosperity. Trump, the ultimate capitalist, took nearly the opposite view. "For the most part," he frequently said, "you can't respect people because most people aren't worthy of respect."[21]

He admitted that his two guiding principles in business were "Always get even" and "Hit back harder than you were hit."[22] In a 2005 speech in Denver, he told the audience that he "loved losers because they make me feel so good about myself."[23] He also insisted that good business leaders should trust no one, good employees in particular. "Be paranoid," he advised, "because they are gonna try to fleece you."[24] Finally, he counseled, "Get even. If somebody screws you, screw 'em back ten times over. At least you can feel good about it. Boy, do I feel good."[25]

This was a favorite theme. Vengeance. Throughout his life, he would unashamedly speak of vengeance as a virtue, nearly as a necessity for success. In his book *Think Big*, he devoted an entire sixteen-page chapter to "Revenge." "I love getting even when I get screwed by someone—yes, it is true. . . . Always get even. When you are in business you need to get even with people who screw you. You need to screw them back fifteen times harder . . . go for the jugular, attack them in spades!"[26] He lived by this rule, treated both the powerful and the defenseless accordingly, and sent more than a few competitors reeling from the market after they received the full Trump treatment.

He had his friends and allies but even they were often skittish. One business partner admitted, "I never at any time liked Donald personally, but that never had anything to do with whether he was the right person."[27] He fell out often with associates and spent hours recounting the grudge matches and insult-fests that dotted his career. He was, in adulthood, much as he had been at New York Military Academy—too competitive for close friends, often alone in his consuming ambition.

But where was God in all of this? Where were the religious lessons his mother had worked to embed in his heart? Where was the imprint of Norman Vincent Peale that would later move the famous preacher to claim Trump as his "greatest student"? Where was the fruit of those hours in church and in chapel at NYMA?

The truth is that for at least the first five decades of Donald Trump's life, there was little evidence of a defining Christian faith. Instead, his religion was power, vengeance, and, notably, himself. He seemed not to know that the ideal of revenge to which he devoted so much time and an entire chapter of a book was contrary to the teaching of the religion he said he served. He did not know or did not care that truth mattered in his faith, that his preference for "truthful hyperbole"—an "innocent form of exaggeration . . . and a very effective form of promotion"—was little more than lying and was forbidden by his religion.[28] It was the same with his sexual mores, with his language, with his business ethics, and with his lack of evident concern for the will of an all-knowing God.

When a former girlfriend was asked by a reporter if she would ever return to Trump, she said, "If a miracle happens and Donald finds God—I'm there."[29] There were many like her who loved Trump and respected his achievements but wished for a better man. They all waited in vain for him to appear.

There did come in time, though, a softening in religious matters; not necessarily a conversion or a dramatic turnaround, but a softening. It came through the influence of some unusual people in his life, and it is important because it helped fashion his appeal to religious conservatives in the 2016 election.

First, though, in order to understand this shift, we must understand the religion that Trump had already embraced. It was the religion that Norman Vincent Peale taught him, that he put into practice, and that is behind much of the Donald Trump the world has come to know. It is a faith that has largely failed him as both a public and a private man but is important to know both for what it produced in his life and for what the change meant when it eventually came.

5 | Peale

I am a believer in positive thinking. A big believer. But I'm also
a big believer in guarding against a downside, because the
upside will take care of itself. I've always said that.

Donald Trump[1]

When we search for evidence of religious faith in the lives of
prominent people, we tend to rely upon externals. We want
connections to mosques, churches, and temples. We listen for
tales of bar mitzvahs and baptisms, of christenings and confirma-
tions. We hope for dramatic altar calls to rival the spectacle of Paul
on the Damascus Road.

Yet these formal expressions may tell us little of the soul. They
may reveal nothing of the imprint of religious ideas or the imagination inflamed by faith. In fact, they could serve to conceal the heart
and so cause us to miss entirely what we hope to know of the man
or woman as a religious being.

Theologian Paul Tillich urged a different approach. He suggested
that if we want to know a person's true religion, we ought to ask
about their "ultimate concern." By this he meant that what consumes
a person's thoughts, what dominates their conversations, what comes

first in their calendar and checkbook, that for which he or she is willing to live or perhaps even to die—this is their religion no matter what their formal associations with religion may be.

Tillich gives us a tool that is particularly helpful in an age like ours that prizes spirituality over traditional religion. Americans are not a people who accept religion unaltered from our ancestors. Instead, we do religion like we do jazz. We customize. We refashion. We curate the old religions into new faiths of our own. In short, we remake religion in our own image. The old labels no longer apply. The old words take on new meaning. The only way to know a person's religion, then, is to know the ultimate concerns that align his or her life and give it purpose.

This approach is especially helpful in trying to understand the religion of Donald Trump. He was raised a Presbyterian, yet we search in vain for the imprint of that faith on Trump's life now. He can become weepy when speaking of his praying mother and the religious training of his youth, yet he has lived the life of a celebrated hedonist. Critics claim he has no faith at all. Supporters claim his religion is too personal to know. Cynics claim he has no faith he cannot put to political use.

Tillich rescues us. He urges us to ask: What is Donald Trump's "ultimate concern"? What dominates his conversation, galvanizes his energies, sets his priorities, and makes him the man he is? The answers come readily from Trump nearly every time he speaks: "self," "winning," "being rich," and "being the best."

These may not seem like religious terms, but they lead us directly to the true religion of Donald Trump and to the man who imprinted that religion upon his soul: Norman Vincent Peale.

This is precisely what Trump himself has been telling us for years. The only man other than his father whom Trump has ever called a mentor is Norman Vincent Peale. The man who called Trump "his greatest student of all time" was Norman Vincent Peale. He was

Trump's spiritual father. He was Trump's mentor from his earliest days. He was the man who fashioned the ultimate concerns that now define the Trump we know.

To understand Donald Trump, then, we must understand the life and the message of Norman Vincent Peale.

We should picture a teenage boy standing in the rotunda of the Ohio State House sometime around the start of World War I. He is skinny, wide-eyed, and dressed like most other small-town Ohio farm boys of his age. He has the manner of a loner, of a sensitive soul more at ease alone than in a bruising crowd. Still, there is a gentle determination about him. He lives in an age that expects him to "make something of himself," and so he harbors ambitions he cannot always admit even to himself.

In the rotunda, he stands before monuments to men like Ulysses S. Grant, William T. Sherman, Philip Sheridan, and William McKinley. He is enthralled, inspired. He lingers before each image. Then he notices what another boy might not. There is a bare space near these monuments. This stirs his imagination. Years later, he would write of this moment:

> My fond ambition was that some day this niche would be occupied by a statue of Norman Vincent Peale, another of Ohio's Jewels, an immortal political figure of the Buckeye State. I didn't exactly aim for the Presidency, but I was not unaware that in those days Ohio was known as the "Mother of Presidents."[2]

Such was the sense of calling to greater things that burned in the heart of young Norman Vincent Peale. Yet there was little about his life at the time that signaled greatness.

He was born in Bowersville, Ohio, on May 31, 1898. His father was the type of Methodist preacher who converted drunks, rescued prostitutes, and held lengthy, sweaty, passionate revival meetings around the Midwest. His mother was intelligent, opinionated, and hardworking. She wanted her son to be a preacher and Norman knew it every day of his life.

He would speak of his childhood home as a place of joy all his life. He remembered his parents as the happiest of people, family gatherings as filled with excitement and love. This all may have been true, but there was something even then that was biting into his soul. He was beset by an inexplicable but debilitating sense of inferiority. This kept him from speaking well, moved him to the shy edge of every crowd, and robbed him of confidence. He thought he knew its source. He wrote in adulthood:

> I was set apart as a different breed, forced always to carry the banner of the church, not able to be just like every other boy. It wasn't that I wanted to do any wrong or unworthy thing but to carry in gay and careless childhood so heavy a responsibility did not seem fair and it served to deepen an already sensitive inferiority complex.[3]

He was also grieved by the way the Methodist church mistreated his father. It is a grief familiar to the children of clergy. The constant moves from town to town, the low pay, the churchy politics, and the bitter disregard by denominational officials made Norman ache for his hero/father. He had once been forced to watch while the local banker haughtily handed his father a small stipend and said, "Do you think your sermon justifies this?" Norman took the humiliation to heart.

Both his personal insecurities and his revulsion for church politics sent Norman in search of answers that were outside of the mainstream. He attended Ohio Wesleyan, where professors urged him toward the works of William James, Ralph Waldo Emerson, and Marcus Aurelius. From James he learned the virtue of "healthy-mindedness" and the power of disciplines to remake the personality. From Emerson he learned the power of "self-reliance," of a man's ability to make his life what he envisioned it to be. From Marcus Aurelius he learned the value of mental disciplines and the power of attitudes to shape a life. Each of these moved him toward pursuit of personal power and away from institutional and traditional religion.

In 1921, he left Ohio to attend Boston University School of Theology for seminary training. He hated it. He was no longer in a Midwestern and Methodist world. He was in Boston, the bastion of New England intellectualism, and he found it an ill fit. He found the theological liberalism and social gospel ideas then swirling about far too ethereal, too untethered to life as lived each day by men and women walking the streets. He once complained on a seminary questionnaire that the school was giving him no "knowledge of the present."

> There is too much philosophy here—we need a good grounding in philosophy to be sure but oftentimes the main interest appears to be directed toward exalting the ideas of Borden P. Bowne et al. I feel that we need a greater stress on the practical work of the ministry. The world needs more preachers rather than philosophers important as they are.[4]

He was no scholar and preferred the personal and practical aspects of religion to the abstract and the social aspects his seminary emphasized. He heard a lecture by Emile Coue in which the statement "Every day in every way I'm getting better and better" was urged upon him. He liked it. It fit with all that James, Emerson, and Marcus Aurelius had taught him. It was practical. It was inspirational. It framed a state of mind that in turn framed reality. This was what Peale was looking for.

His father had helped to move him in this direction. During Norman's first summer home from seminary, he had been asked to fill in for an ailing preacher. He wrote his sermon in the only way he knew—in the style of the Boston preachers and professors. He gave it his best and then asked his father what he thought. "My advice

75

would be to take it out back and burn it," the elder Peale said bluntly. "The way to the human heart is through simplicity." It was a turning point.

After seminary, he served in several New York churches and, remembering his father's rough-hewn advice, began to hit his stride as an orator. He found the confidence to move away from the pulpit and to preach without notes. He allowed himself to be more theatrical in his preaching, which in turn allowed him to remake timeworn Bible stories into tales of inspiration. His church members found him a refreshing change from the staid clergy of his day.

He also learned from his congregations. Many of his members were businesspeople and industry leaders. By watching them closely, he learned much about the craft of salesmanship, of promotion, and of moving customers—or was it lost souls?—to commitment. He was not ashamed to speak of preaching and selling as the same thing and to adopt the methods of business. The language of Wall Street adorned his church signs and bulletins: "Largest Vested Children's Choir in the State," "Syracuse's Youngest Preacher," "The Greatest University Audience in America," "Greatest Choir in Empire State."

He also began to innovate theologically. Though he would claim throughout his life that he had never abandoned the born-again gospel of his Methodist upbringing, he was so eager to find language to persuade his business-oriented congregations and was so desperate to inspire a Great Depression–plagued people that he lessened biblical theology in his sermons in favor of motivational psychology. He had come to believe that a person of normal intelligence had the power to remake himself through thought and deed into whatever he wanted to become. He spoke of the Sermon on the Mount as a "practical program for personality building."[5]

His original thinking and rhetorical skills won him a reputation as a rising young star. In 1932, just eight years after he graduated from seminary, he was asked to lead the historic Marble Collegiate Church in New York City. This prestigious congregation dated from

1628 and offered Peale opportunity to do what he loved doing most: preach. He would not be burdened with administrative duties, he would be paid well, and, since attendance had been declining at the church for some time, there was opportunity for an ambitious, energetic young minister to show what he could do. Peale accepted the invitation.

He led the church for most of the next half century, fashioning it into one of the nation's premier congregations. On his first Sunday, he spoke to barely two hundred souls. A year later, the congregation had grown to nine hundred. By the 1950s, that number had increased to over four thousand.

Yet it was his refashioning of Christian truth that made him among the most famous and controversial religious figures of his age. Looking back upon this time decades later, Peale's own father described his son's theology as "a composite of Science of Mind [New Thought], metaphysics, Christian Science, medical and psychological practice, Baptist Evangelism, Methodist witnessing, and solid Dutch Reformed Calvinism."[6]

It is the casual presence of "New Thought" in this list that is most surprising. Usually regarded as occult by mainstream Christians, the New Thought or mind science movements taught that human thoughts could "manifest" themselves in the real world. This was the teaching of Phineas Quimby, mentor to Mary Baker Eddy, the founder of the Christian Science Church. Followers lived healthy, fulfilled lives by thinking with the "Divine Mind" rather than with the "Mortal Mind." This amounted to disbelieving in the reality of sin and disease and believing instead in the reality of health and wholeness. As a person thought, so he or she became.

We know this better in our own day as an emphasis of Oprah Winfrey and the phenomenally popular book *The Secret*. In 2006, Australian television producer Rhonda Byrne compiled traditional New Thought themes into a slickly packaged book and video series she called *The Secret*. Released in March 2006, the set broke sales records for its genre. By Christmas that year, it ranked in the top five of Amazon's Christmas bestsellers.

On February 7, 2007, Oprah hosted Byrne on her daily talk show and could not have offered more effusive praise for *The Secret*. She told her audience that as she opened the book and DVD set, "I took God out of the box."

Byrne explained on the show that *The Secret* was nothing more than the Law of Attraction, which meant simply, "Thoughts become things." This was New Thought teaching captured in three words. "So what you're saying," Oprah excitedly asked, "is that we all . . . create our own circumstances by the choices that we make and the choices that we make are fueled by our thoughts? So our thoughts are the most powerful things that we have here on Earth?" Byrne said yes.

Turning to her audience, Winfrey declared, "It means that everything that happens to you, good and bad, you are attracting to yourself. It's something that I really have believed in for years, that the energy you put out into the world is always gonna be coming back to you. That's the basic principle."[7] Though neither Byrne nor Winfrey mentioned Phineas Quimby or Norman Vincent Peale, they were perfectly expressing the teaching of these two religious pioneers.

Peale taught this same law of attraction in typically practical, homespun terms. "If you get mad at your wife," he preached to vast audiences, "something is sure to happen to you; you will bring it on yourself. She won't have to do a thing but sit and wait for it." This was little different from Oprah Winfrey's trendy concept of *karma*: "The energy you put out into the world is always gonna be coming back to you."

What distinguished Peale was his attempt to wed New Thought and mind science to the Christian gospel. In his 1938 book *You Can Win*, for example, he emphasized traditional Christian themes of sin, struggle, and a life surrendered to God. "Simply stated," he explained, "it means: A man has no power in himself, he is weak;

his will is weak; he wants to gain a victory but does not have the strength."[8] That strength, he insisted, came only from God.

This call to rely on God alone did not seem to fit with the idea that a person's thoughts could determine his or her life. "I am what I think I am" and "I am what God makes me" are two different truths. Peale preached them both and they often led him to the type of nonspecific language he used in *You Can Win*. "Life has a key," he wrote, "and to find that key is to be assured of success in the business of living. . . . To win over the world a man must get hold of some power in his inward or spiritual life which will never let him down."[9]

Peale wanted to champion both the fiery Methodist gospel and New Thought empowerment at the same time. This produced an uncomfortable tension in his life, in his preaching, and in his reputation. He was eager to reach businessmen and trendy New Yorkers with a snazzy gospel of personal empowerment. He also wanted to call men to salvation through Jesus Christ as his father and generations of Methodist circuit riders before him had done. He became a master of the balancing act required to grasp the one without entirely losing the other.

A later senior minister at Marble Collegiate Church, Reverend Michael Brown, believed that there were two Peales. In lectures before the wider world, Peale would proclaim, "You can if you think you can." From the pulpit of his church, he would declare this same truth but in slightly different, more biblical terms: "You can do all things through Christ, who strengthens you."[10] Both the Christian Peale and the New Thought Peale were profoundly influential in American culture.

This was in large part due to the release of *The Power of Positive Thinking* in 1952. The book not only made Peale the most famous Protestant clergyman in the world but also established him as a religious innovator—some said a religious cult leader. It landed on bookshelves at just the right time and helped define an age. Americans began learning of the plain little volume a few months before Dwight Eisenhower defeated Adlai E. Stevenson in the race for the White House. The suffocating gloom of the Cold War was spreading over the world. It had already been six years since Winston Churchill warned of an "Iron Curtain" descending upon Europe. Americans were ripe for inspiration, for a gospel of personal empowerment, and for distraction.

Peale offered all of this and in the simplest of terms. His chapters included titles like "Expect the Best and Get It," "How to Create Your Own Happiness," "Inflow of New Thoughts Can Remake You," "I Don't Believe in Defeat," and "How to Get People to Like You." Asked about his book's point of view, he answered, "good overbalances evil." Asked for a biblical verse to support his message, he quoted Jesus: "Be of good cheer. I have overcome the world."[11]

The book was an astonishing success. It stayed at the top of the bestseller lists for three years. By the end of the Eisenhower era, it had sold two million copies.[12] By 1974, it had sold three million in hardback alone.[13] The plain little volume has easily reached sales beyond the twenty million mark since.

The Power of Positive Thinking treated a traditional American theme in nontraditional terms. As early as 1831, visiting Frenchman Alexis de Tocqueville had complained of American preachers that "It is often difficult to ascertain from their discourse whether the principal object of religion is to procure eternal felicity in the other-world or prosperity in this."[14] That Peale offered success as a by-product of faith in God was nothing new. What was innovative was Peale's insistence that every person can learn to use his or her thoughts to shape his or her life. This had been the province of cults and psychics for a century or more. Peale mainstreamed it, baptizing it before an eager post-WWII America.

His vocabulary and phrasing may be familiar to us now, living as we do in an age of motivational-speak, self-help, and positive imaging. Yet it would be helpful to list some of Peale's more representative statements in order to better understand both his pioneering concepts and the way he tried to merge them with traditional Christianity. These are the statements from *The Power of Positive Thinking* that swirled in the mind of Peale's "greatest student," Donald Trump.

When you expect the best, you release a magnetic force in your mind which by a law of attraction tends to bring the best to you. But if you expect the worst, you release from your mind the power of repulsion which tends to force the best from you. It is amazing how a sustained expectation of the best sets in motion forces which cause the best to materialize. (p. 90)

What you 'image' (imagine) may ultimately become a fact if held mentally with sufficient faith. (p. 121)

When you elevate your thoughts into the area of visualized attainment you look down on your problems rather than from below up at them and thus you get a much more encouraging view of them. Always come up over your problems. Never approach a problem below. (p. 168)

"Attitudes are more important than facts." Any fact facing us, however difficult, even seemingly hopeless, is not so important as our attitude toward that fact. (p. 20)

Formulate and stamp indelibly on your mind a mental picture of yourself as succeeding. Hold this picture tenaciously. Never permit it to fade. Your mind will seek to develop this picture. Never think of yourself as failing; never doubt the reality of the mental image. So always picture "success" no matter how badly things seem to be going at the moment. (p. 22)

To the degree to which your attitude shifts from negative to positive the mastery touch will come to you. Then, with assurance, you can say to yourself under any and all circumstances and mean it, "I don't believe in defeat." (p. 107)

If you mentally visualize and affirm and reaffirm your assets and keep your thoughts on them, emphasizing them to the fullest extent, you will rise out of any difficulty regardless of what it may be. Your inner powers will reassert themselves and, with the help of God, lift you from defeat to victory. (p. 21)

Peale's supporters celebrated him for rearticulating the message of Jesus for the modern world. Most of those who read his books, magazines, newspaper columns, and even greeting cards, or who listened to his radio broadcasts or attended his lectures would have agreed. Others saw his work as more sinister. One scholar called *The Power of Positive Thinking* a "New Thought classic."[15] The term used most often by critics was "cult." They described Peale as leading "The Cult of Reassurance," "The Cult of Positive Thinking," "The Cult of Easy Religion," and "The Cult of Happiness."[16]

He was stung by the criticism hurled at his bestseller. He had long lived in a tug-of-war between historic Christianity and mind science. Now that tug-of-war was no longer just in his own thoughts. Millions were joining on both sides, each pulling violently in their preferred direction.

Peale insisted he was still a servant of "the old-fashioned gospel." Yet when an article he had written appeared in the journal *Science of the Mind*, he told friends, "They think I am one of them, but I am not. Actually I am not opposed to it."[17]

He was clearly a man in conflict with himself, as he explained later in an interview.

I'm a conservative, and I will tell you exactly what I mean by that. I mean that I have accepted the Lord Jesus Christ as my personal Savior. I mean that I believe my sins are forgiven by the atoning work of grace on the cross. . . . Now, I'll tell you something else . . . I personally love and understand this way of stating the Christian gospel. But I am absolutely and thoroughly convinced that it is my mission never to use this language in trying to communicate with the audience that has been given me.[18]

If Peale would not use the language of the Christian gospel before his audiences, then what was left was the New Thought/mind science confidence in thoughts shaping reality, in victories won and prosperity assured through believing in oneself enough. It was an emphasis Peale did not hide. The first two sentences in *The Power of Positive Thinking* are "Believe in yourself! Have faith in your abilities."

The book helped to make him a cultural force. By 1957, he was reaching a weekly audience of thirty million people. This was in a country with half the population of today. His syndicated newspaper columns attracted ten million readers a week. The *Guideposts* magazine he had founded reached five hundred thousand subscribers. His sermons were sent to 150,000 people worldwide.[19]

He had long been outspoken about politics. In 1942, the *New York Sun* celebrated him as

[A] vigorous assailant of the New Deal, preaching eloquent sermons against bureaucracy, official bungling, mudding and meddling, invasion of individual rights, wrecking of American traditions, coddling the unemployed, providing relief for the undeserving, knuckling to union labor, the menace of a third term, in fact, the entire category of New Deal sins as he sees them.[20]

With his publishing success granting him greater visibility, Peale used his broadening platform to shape American politics with ever increasing ferocity.

He was almost religiously devoted to the virtues of the free market and said he wanted to wed American churches to capitalism. This set him in opposition to nearly everything Franklin Roosevelt attempted in his New Deal. Harry Truman disgusted him. He furiously opposed John F. Kennedy's campaign for president, believing Kennedy's Catholicism required complete submission to a foreign state: the Vatican.

He was famously devoted to Richard Nixon, whom he claimed was "the greatest positive thinker of our times."[21] He traveled to Vietnam to visit American troops at Nixon's request, officiated at the wedding of Julie Nixon and David Eisenhower, and stood by the beleaguered president during the darkest days of Watergate. Always at home in the Republican fold, Peale received the Presidential Medal of Freedom from the hands of Ronald Reagan in 1984.

It was also in that year that Peale's legacy was playing itself out in American culture. A 1984 Gallup poll revealed that "as many people were involved in positive thinking seminars as belonged to the Methodist Church."[22] Upon hearing the news, the eighty-six-year-old Peale seemed pleased. Calmly, firmly, he said, "I belong to this."[23]

The problem with Norman Vincent Peale was exactly the breadth of message that made him so popular. Those who wanted to know more of God and his son Jesus Christ, more of historic Christianity, could hear enough in Peale's preaching to hold their interest. Those who wanted to be generally religious without being distinctly Christian could also find encouragement in Peale's message. Yet those trapped in a self-centered age would hear from Peale the same call to confidence in self, the same certainty that people can fashion their own destiny, and the same assurance that prosperity is the measure of a life well lived that other, non-Christian gurus of the age offered. Indeed, it was difficult at times to distinguish the message of Norman Vincent Peale from the spirit of the times, the idols of the age that were proving to be without power to satisfy men's souls.

This brings us back to Donald Trump. He is a maddening combination of Christian memory and unrelenting self-centeredness, belief in the power of the positive and an even greater belief in the power of himself, certainty about his importance in the world and nagging, inexplicable insecurity.

This is all consistent with the imprint of Norman Vincent Peale upon his life. Peale offered him a religion of empowerment, not of transformation. Trump took from this that it is God's will to carry him further in the direction he was already going. He did not understand from his time under Peale's ministry that God empowers a man only after he remakes him.

Does Donald Trump have a religious faith? Yes. It is a faith he has carried with him for many years. It is a faith he holds dear. It is a faith that will guide him while he is president. The problem for both Trump and the nation, though, is that this faith is the one he learned from Norman Vincent Peale.

6 White

Paula White is a beautiful person both inside and out.

Donald Trump[1]

t all began with an unexpected phone call one day in 2002. She had heard of Donald Trump, of course. She knew him by reputation and had seen him on TV. That was all. He was the last person she expected would ring her phone and start up a conversation.

He was energized as he spoke that day. He had seen her on television giving a talk called "The Value of Vision." He had heard many speeches about vision in his life, but this one was different. It was practical. She had not merely urged her viewers to have a vision for their lives but she had challenged them to execute as well. They would have to set goals. They would have to learn discipline. They would have to combine trust in God with hard work and wise management. Trump loved it. It reminded him of the preaching of his mentor, Norman Vincent Peale.

In his excitement, Trump quoted huge portions of what she had said. Then he quoted from some of her other teachings. He had obviously been paying attention. This impressed her. She received many compliments for her speaking, as preachers and speechmakers often do, but she preached for effect and loved it when people showed they had absorbed, that they were more than just entertained. Trump had listened. He had retained. There was some depth in this man.

He was a confusing mixture. He was certainly the man on the magazine covers—the tough New York real estate magnate who destroyed rivals, turned pursuing women into blood sport, and was obsessed with self-promotion. Yet he was also a man with a keen spiritual hunger. He watched television preachers by the hour, often late into the night. He was fascinated by them, drawn by their power and the way they spoke about God. For years, he had admired Jimmy Swaggart and Billy Graham. He loved the preaching of David Jeremiah too. There were others, but he had never seen anyone quite like the woman he was speaking to on the phone now, the unusual preacher named Paula White.

"Listen," he said, "if you are ever in New York, stop by. My wife and I would love to meet you."

She explained that she was often in New York. She conducted Bible studies for some of the Yankees baseball players and would be delighted to visit him and meet his wife.

Not long after this initial conversation, she visited Trump in his office. He introduced her to his staff and showed her around his marbled headquarters. The Trump offices are a raucous place, with numerous clusters of people standing around while others come and go at disorienting speed. His door is never closed. He likes the energy, the commotion. He feeds on movement and the buzz in the room when talented people work.

When she could get his attention, she said the words that began it all. "I don't need anything from you. I don't want anything from you. But if I can help you, I will." He had seldom been spoken to like this. He was one of the most powerful men in America and most people stumbled over themselves seeking something from him. This woman wanted nothing but offered to help where she could. It impressed him.

She soon became the closest thing to a pastor he had in his life at the time. He had not attended Marble Collegiate Church regularly since his hero, Norman Vincent Peale, had died in 1993 and a new minister had taken over. He was adrift spiritually, which often left him victim to the dark side of his nature. She recommended books, prayed for him and his family, counseled his children, and became a cool, relatable minister to many of his staff. Her books were strewn about the Trump corporate offices. Her impressions from God were heeded. Her prayers for endangered marriages, errant children, and new business ventures were cherished. She became an unofficial chaplain to the man, to the family, to the company, and, ultimately, to the president of the United States.

She was, by all accounts including hers, an unusual choice. She was obviously a gifted woman. At the time she met Trump, she was the copastor of a thriving megachurch and there was hardly a moment of the day when she was not on some television channel somewhere in the world. She was on an ascent. Some said it was her "sister vibe" that made her so popular. She had also been through hard times. This heightened her appeal. She didn't just preach what she knew, like most ministers; she preached about the wrenching seasons she had been through and about how she became a better person in them. Her African-American audiences adored her for this. The editors of *Ebony* magazine declared of her, "You know you're on to something new and significant when the most popular woman preacher on the Black Entertainment Network is a white woman."[2]

She also had her critics. She seemed almost designed to offend the straightlaced and religiously uptight. She was pretty and shapely and sometimes dressed so as to make her gifts known, even when preaching. She spoke in a racing torrent of words that made some in her audience ask how she breathed. She was also self-educated, which was admirable but which meant she often made mistakes. She regularly dropped bad grammar and frequently mispronounced words, a common problem for the self-educated. Harry Truman was known for it all his life. He had read nearly all the three thousand books in the Independence, Missouri, library during his youth, which meant he knew the meanings of words he had never heard pronounced. Even after he had reached the Oval Office, his mangling of terms would make the Harvard and Yale boys wince. Paula White did the same.

Those close to her said these traits belied her innate intelligence. She labored to overcome gaps in her knowledge. In spare moments, she was as likely to be reading a ponderous tome of theology as she was her Bible. It is one of the marks of those who have risen in part through the power of self-education. They never stop. They know that they don't know all they need to know, and they have every intention of making up the deficit. In this, as in most arenas, there is no substitute for hard work.

All of this surely endeared her to Donald Trump. He liked that she was not one of the ponderous and self-important clergy, that she took God seriously but very little else. He liked that she spoke with a conviction he recognized about purpose, about victory, about outstripping the demons that come in the night, and about a Jesus who understands the deformities in people's souls. If he noticed that listening to her preach was like drinking from a fire hose or that she made grammatical mistakes, he didn't care. He had fought the experts and the know-it-alls his whole life. He would choose the little blonde preacher woman with all her flaws. She had one hand on God.

She was also a woman with a past, and this, too, must have made her a bit more believable to Donald Trump. Paula White was born in Tupelo, Mississippi, in 1966. Her parents separated when she was five years old, and her father committed suicide soon after. There was a suicide note. The man was fighting personal demons he could not overcome. His death left Paula, her brother, and her mother impoverished, which thrust her mother into an alcoholic swirl.

Concerned friends and babysitters stepped in to provide the care Paula's hardworking, hard-drinking mother could not, and this is when the sexual abuse began. It lasted for seven years and nearly destroyed Paula. The experience ravaged her soul and left her the victim of a host of addictions. "I was sexually and physically abused numerous times in horrific ways," White explained years later. "Psychiatrists and psychologists told me that, given what happened to me in those early years of my childhood, I should have been institutionalized for the rest of my life."[3]

She converted to Christianity in 1984 when a friend challenged her to consider the purposes of God for her life. Shortly after, she reported an experience that would shape her long after:

> When I was just eighteen years old, the Lord gave me a vision that every time I opened my mouth and declared the Word of the Lord, there was a manifestation of His Spirit where people were either healed, delivered, or saved. When I shut my mouth, they fell off into utter darkness and God spoke to me and said, "I called you to preach the gospel."[4]

She had already married and borne a child by this time. Soon after her conversion, her husband divorced her. Paula moved on, raised her son, started a cleaning service to pay her bills, and volunteered as a janitor at the church she attended. All was not well, though. "As a young Christian, no matter how I looked at my life, from every direction I saw a gigantic mess," she recounted years later. "When I examined my world, the sum total of my life seemed to be brokenness. Unkept promises and shattered dreams had left me in despair. My unwise choices had produced devastating consequences. I had very little to offer God."[5]

Not long after, she met Randy White, a third-generation pastor/ evangelist in the Church of God denomination. This had become Paula's denomination too, and as she spent time with Randy she realized the two had much in common. Both had known broken-ness. Both had known poverty. Both had been divorced, and this in a church that viewed divorce as nearly the unpardonable sin.

Inspired largely by his friendship, she began discovering her gifts. Her hard-won love for Scripture began feeding a passion for teaching. People admired her intensity, her willingness to dig out the gems of the Bible, and her informal, self-deprecating manner when she taught. To her, it was all confirmation of a calling.

She married Randy White in 1989 and the two moved to Tampa, Florida. In 1991, they founded what would become Without Walls International Church. The grand name of later years belies the beginning. The church struggled in its early days and met in a variety of locations but finally began to grow. By late 1991, seven hundred people called Randy and Paula their pastors. By 1999, there were nearly five thousand people attending the church. By 2006, an astonishing twenty thousand gathered every week, making the couple among the best-known religious leaders in the world.

This was during the time when Donald Trump was just getting to know Paula. She was the gifted copastor of a megachurch. She was mentored by the esteemed African-American pastor T. D. Jakes, who seemed to know she would be a sensation at his huge international conferences. She had also begun broadcasting *The Paula White Show*, which would eventually air on nine different television networks. This was the female preacher Donald Trump met in 2002 and grew to admire.

If he had merely wanted to associate with a rising star, he would have opportunity for disappointment. In the ten years after he met White, she and her husband divorced, she resigned as pastor of her troubled church, her stepdaughter died, she was investigated for financial misdealings by members of the United States Senate, and critics loudly charged she was a heretic and a charlatan.

Trump remained a friend. He had grown to trust her and rely upon her sense of God's will for his life. He was also fascinated by how she rebuilt her life after so much devastation. She continued to preach, continued to broadcast, and continued to write books that seemed to impact lives. Trump could hear evidence for this in the stories told by his own staff members. Eventually, White became the pastor of another megachurch, New Destiny Christian Center in Apopka, Florida. She also married again, this time to Jonathan Cain, drummer for the rock group Journey.

Had it gone no further, had she simply remained the famous preacher friend to the more famous real estate magnate and reality TV star, most Americans would have little need for knowing even the broad outlines of Paula White's life. Yet she stepped onto the pages of American history when Donald Trump decided to run for president of the United States in 2015. Indeed, it is not going too far to say that Paula White helped deliver the Oval Office into Donald Trump's hands.

This influence beyond the spiritual alone began in 2011, when Trump considered running for president again. He had already announced once before, in 2000. White was the national religious leader he knew best and he needed her help. Would she invite ministers from around the country to meet with him? He needed to change his image with the clergy and he wanted to hear their concerns, to understand their perspectives on the upheavals of the day. White agreed. A few inconsequential meetings were held. Soon, though, Trump began having doubts. He asked White what she thought of his run for office. "I don't think it's the time," she said. "I don't either," he agreed.

In 2015, a Trump intent upon winning the White House asked for White's help again. Would she organize meetings of pastors? Would she ask them to advise him and pray for him? This is what Trump wanted, and White was eager to comply.

What happened next would help to shape the course of American history, and it occurred because of a shift that had already transpired in White. She had begun her Christian life as a Pentecostal. She liked the passion, the emphasis on the power of God to change lives, and the confidence that God still gave gifts of spiritual insight and healing to his people. She felt at home among them and would forever be thankful for what they embedded in her life. She was still shaped by her Pentecostal roots when she began pastoring and stepped onto an international stage.

In time, though, she began to realize the severe limitations of religious denominations. They could become narrow, tradition-bound, and divisive. Wars over denominational distinctions had nearly killed off biblical Christianity many times throughout church history, she came to believe. As she spoke around the world and met religious leaders from a variety of backgrounds, she began to grieve over the divisions among Christians worldwide and to understand the valuable contributions of believers far different from those she had known. She soon realized what she had to do. She publicly declared herself a "free agent." Though grateful for her Pentecostal roots, she would be a Christian leader at large, affirming the cause of Christ in whatever form it might take.

This newfound openness had a direct impact upon how she helped Donald Trump run for president. Had she thought only as a Pentecostal, had she introduced him only to that brand of religious leader, the meetings she organized might have been warm and informative, but they would not have connected Trump to the greater mass of religious conservatives. Her gift to his campaign was her reach to religious leaders far different from those she had known before.

The first most Americans learned of White's meetings was when they saw photos of well-known televangelists surrounding Trump in prayer meetings and "laying hands" on him. The first of such meetings was in Dallas in September 2015. Among those involved were Kenneth Copeland, David Jeremiah, Rabbi Kirt Schneider, Bishop Darrell Scott, and Jan Crouch of Trinity Broadcasting Network. In a brief talk, Trump assured the ministers he would defend religious liberty, support Israel, and work to defeat ISIS. It was just what many of them had hoped to hear.

Most of the ministers in this initial meeting represented White's home turf, though. What began to make a national difference were her efforts at a wider reach. She worked to connect Trump to Southern Baptist leaders such as Robert Jeffress of First Baptist Church in Dallas and Richard Land, president of Southern Evangelical Seminary and former head of the Baptist's Ethics and Religious Liberty Commission. Baptists have historically been suspicious of Pentecostals and their Charismatic descendants, but Jeffress and Land—along with hundreds like them nationwide—began to trust and love White. Soon they started helping her.

She scheduled meetings that included nearly every variation of Protestantism. This was relatively easy once a few successful gatherings had occurred and she had won endorsements from several prominent Protestant leaders. White went further, though. She urged Trump to meet with Roman Catholics, and if she did not know an important bishop or archbishop herself, she found those who did. She also involved Orthodox priests, a harder achievement for a female television preacher and former Pentecostal. It paid off. So did involving Jewish rabbis and even a few sympathetic Muslim leaders.

The impact of these meetings is hard to exaggerate. The education Trump received not only prioritized his campaign but is certain to shape his presidency for as long as it lasts. It was in these gatherings of religious leaders that Trump learned about the restrictions of the Johnson Amendment, the sufferings of Christians and Jews in the Middle East, the attempted kidnapping of Islam by extremists, the duplicity of Palestinian leadership, the devastation of gang violence, and the scourge of poverty in some of America's inner cities.

He also heard much about the threat of the Obama administration to traditional religion. More than one pastor complained of the Supreme Court's *Obergefell v. Hodges* ruling that legalized same-sex marriage nationwide. Obama supported it and had no mercy for those who disagreed, Trump was told. Numerous clergy made sure Trump understood what Obamacare meant for pro-life Americans. He heard from Catholics about federal pressure to perform abortions in Catholic hospitals and from evangelicals about what the owners of the Hobby Lobby chain of stores endured under Obamacare for refusing to include abortion services in their employee health-care plan.

These gatherings of diverse religious leaders also connected Trump to largely undeployed battalions of religious conservatives. This was an angry tribe, one that felt despised by its own federal government and bullied by the Obama administration. On issues that ranged from immigration to contending with ISIS, from protecting the traditional family to assuring their children's economic future, these Americans perceived the Obama administration not just as incompetent but as a foe. They were furious. They were eager for change. They told themselves they were not searching for a pastor but for a president who could restore what had been lost. They would support even a man like Donald Trump if it meant reclaiming their country.

They were encouraged by the most powerful religious leaders in America—the archbishop of Boston, the son of Billy Graham, the top religious broadcasters, and most of the leaders of the fifty largest churches in the nation. It was all an overwhelming success. Donald Trump—he of the three marriages, the casinos, the racist campaign statements, the misquoting of Scripture, and the foul language—won the votes of 81 percent of white evangelicals, more than half of all Roman Catholics, and more than half of all weekly church attenders in the United States.[6]

Much of this was the doing of Paula White. She prayed for Trump publicly and privately, she gave him counsel, and she helped him win the voters that were certainly among those least likely in all the United States to find him a fit. He won by a margin much smaller than the voters she helped draw to him. And she will continue to be an influence. Trump has appointed her the chairwoman of his Evangelical Advisory Council.

She will do in this role what she has done for many years for Donald Trump: explain him. She knows how to frame her religiously clumsy friend in terms that American religious conservatives understand. "If he suddenly came out all religious, that would seem staged to me," she told a reporter. "Donald has never been public about his faith, and when he has tried, it has been futile. It's not his language, but that doesn't mean it's not his heart." What she genuinely believes about Trump is what a huge portion of American conservatives want to hear. "He absolutely has a heart and a hunger and a relationship with God," she assures. "He is a Christian, and he is born again."[7]

Explaining Trump's religion will certainly exact a price. Critics she will always have with her. A Duke University theologian assures that the only reason White has the place that she does in Donald Trump's life is that "She's blonde and cute and perky and endlessly optimistic."[8] Others allege that it is White's emphasis on prosperity in her preaching that endears her to Trump. He loves nothing more than wealth and success. Yet White has been a target before and is likely to outlast her detractors. "I'm not saying there isn't mud on me," she often replies with a smile, "I am just saying that much of it has been thrown on me."[9]

She is, though, nearly the perfect face of religion in the Trump administration. She is gifted but sometimes inarticulate, successful but occasionally naïve, sincere but not infrequently unwise. Yet she is the architect of Donald Trump's influence among religious conservatives. This is no small thing. His bond with them is destined to influence the whole of an American presidency.

PART 3

The Appeal

Donald Trump was carried into the White House by an angry tribe. They felt themselves being sidelined by history and feared their country as they knew it was slipping away. They wanted change, at nearly any cost, and they looked beyond more experienced candidates to set their hopes upon the sharp-tongued, hard-hitting, angry-as-they-were billionaire from New York. He won them by promising to give their country back to them and to win a future for their children. They believed him, largely because he spoke of faith like a crusader, like one who understood religion as a perpetual call to arms.

7 | Johnson

The Johnson Amendment has blocked our pastors and ministers and others from speaking their minds from their own pulpits. If they want to talk about Christianity, if they want to preach, if they want to talk about politics, they're unable to do so. If they want to do it, they take a tremendous risk that they lose their tax-exempt status. All religious leaders should be able to freely express their thoughts and feelings on religious matters, and I will repeal the Johnson Amendment if I am elected President.

Donald Trump[1]

Donald Trump is a fighter. There is no understanding him apart from this truth. He feels himself at his best in the role of combatant. Conflict summons his energies, organizes his thoughts, aligns his allegiances, and clarifies his sense of destiny. Donald Trump is a fighter.

He was mystified, then, by the defeatism he thought he saw in the clergy Paula White arranged for him to meet. He admired their devotion and was drawn by their gifts. Yet their refusal to engage disturbed him. Their faith was under attack in nearly every arena of

American culture. Their own government legislated against them. Still, they would not use their bully pulpits to fight back. He wanted to know why.

When he asked, the ministers who met with him began talking about the Johnson Amendment. Trump had never heard of it. He understood the tactics of the IRS well but was new to the idea that America's preachers were somehow muzzled under threat of their churches losing tax-exempt status. He pressed to know more. Ministers around the country explained at length. Trump grew incensed.

What enraged him was the unjust stifling of religious speech, but there was more. The same IRS restrictions that prevented clergy from taking stands on political issues also prevented them from endorsing candidates. This meant that the ministers who pledged loyalty to Donald Trump in private could not do so publicly. He saw an opportunity both to right what he considered a moral wrong and to unchain a vast army of influential supporters. The Johnson Amendment had to go.

This commitment led to what happened in Dallas on February 26, 2016. Trump's appearance on that date is usually remembered for two occurrences. The first was the announcement that New Jersey governor and former presidential candidate Chris Christie had pledged his support to Trump. The second was a raucous retort to Marco Rubio's claim that Trump was so undone by recent political pressure that he had urinated on himself. Clearly, the 2016 presidential campaign had already become angry and crass. For the nation's religious leaders, though, there was a third and far more important occurrence in Dallas.

During a speech that day, Trump warmed to the topic of religion and then began describing the Johnson Amendment. He briefly explained what it was. He had been schooled by clergy on the matter and had done his own research. He was a quick study. He pledged to see the Johnson Amendment abolished.

Then, surprisingly, Trump called Reverend Robert Jeffress, pastor of the immense and prominent First Baptist Church in Dallas, to the stage. Jeffress had been an early supporter of Trump and the two had spoken often about religious liberty issues, the restrictions of the Johnson Amendment in particular. They briefly spoke of it again on stage and then Trump turned to Jeffress and said, "Pastor, I am going to abolish the Johnson Amendment. And I want you to hold me accountable for this." The watching crowd roared its approval.

It was a typical Trump move. The candidate, perceived by most Americans as among the most secular people ever to seek the presidency, was in the process of transforming himself into a champion of religious liberty. By displaying both his familiarity with the concerns of religious Americans and his eagerness to answer those concerns, Trump could win support from some of the nation's most powerful religious leaders. Through them, he could win millions more. If successful, it would be an astonishing political feat, especially in the minds of those who knew the questionable morality of Trump's past. It worked, and it worked so admirably that it shifted the religious balance in the 2016 presidential race and helped carry Donald Trump into the Oval Office.

The far-reaching Johnson Amendment had its origins in the political machinations of Lyndon Baines Johnson. In 1954, Johnson was a freshman senator from Texas seeking reelection to a second term. He had much to live down, though. Six years before, he had won his Senate race by only 87 votes—a mere 1/100th of 1 percent of the vote. The narrow margin had earned him the nickname "Landslide Lyndon."

It had not helped that he was carried to victory by the last-minute appearance of a mysterious "Box 13" from Duval County, a box that contained two hundred votes for Johnson but only one for his opponent. Much winking and eye-rolling ensued. This was Texas politics, after all. The shenanigans of that election prompted conservative leader William Buckley to quip decades later that though his grandfather had died in 1904, he was possessed of such a strong "sense of civic obligation" that he rose again to vote for Johnson in 1948. Critics charged that the elder Buckley was not the only dead man to vote for Johnson that year.

By 1954, Johnson was facing fierce and concerted opposition. McCarthyism was on the rise and its extreme form of anticommunism made Lyndon Johnson seem hesitant. As he famously told Senate friends, "Joe McCarthy's just a loudmouthed drunk. Hell, he's the sorriest senator up here. . . . But he's riding high now, he's got people scared to death some communist will strangle 'em in their sleep, and anybody who takes him on before the fevers cool—well, you don't get in a pissin' contest with a polecat."[2]

Johnson's attitudes outraged conservatives and stirred some of the nation's most powerful men to action. Much to the concern of the junior senator from Texas, these men sought to shape events through tax-exempt organizations.

Wealthy Texas oilman H. L. Hunt, a strident anticommunist, had founded the Facts Forum. With its radio shows, television programs, books, and magazines, Facts Forum took a hardline approach against communism that made Johnson's more moderate stand look like treason by comparison. Newspaperman Frank Gannett had started the Committee for Constitutional Government, which in a seven-year period distributed eighty-two million pieces of literature and produced over one hundred thousand radio transcripts. Like Facts Forum, Gannett's organization quietly but firmly opposed Lyndon Johnson's return to the Senate.

Political use of these tax-exempt organizations infuriated Johnson. He knew that other members of Congress felt the same. A House Special Committee to Investigate Tax-Exempt Foundations had even held hearings on this rising threat, but nothing of value had come of it.

Johnson wasn't satisfied. He decided to pursue the matter on his own. As he told a friend at the time, "I myself am wondering whether contributions to an organization so actively engaged in politics can be classed as a legitimate corporate expense and I am having this question explored by experts."[3]

He learned that a 1934 amendment to the statutes that governed tax-exempt organizations had originally included the words, "and no substantial part of the activities of which is participation in partisan politics or in carrying on propaganda, or otherwise attempting to influence legislation." In the final version of the bill, the words "participation in partisan politics" were dropped.[4] In Johnson's mind, the teeth had been taken out of the law. He intended to restore them.

On the same day that the House Special Committee to Investigate Tax-Exempt Foundations ended its investigation—July 2, 1954—Johnson rose on the Senate floor. He announced that he intended to offer an amendment to the Internal Revenue Service Code governing political activities by tax-exempt, 501(c)(3) organizations.

What came next would alter the course of religion in America, and it would all be done in a matter of seconds. The *Congressional Record* tells the tale.

Mr. JOHNSON of Texas: Mr. President, I have an amendment at the desk, which I should like to have stated.

The PRESIDING OFFICER: The Secretary will state the amendment.

The CHIEF CLERK: On page 117 of the House bill, in section 501(c) (3), it is proposed to strike out "individuals, and" and insert "individual," and strike out "influence legislation." And insert "influence legislation, and which does not participate in, or intervene in (including the publishing or distributing of statements), any political campaign on behalf of any candidate for public office."

Mr. JOHNSON of Texas: Mr. President, this amendment seeks to extend the provisions of section 501 of the House bill, denying tax-exempt status to not only those people who influence legislation but also to those who intervene in any political campaign on behalf of any candidate for any public office. I have discussed the matter with the chairman of the committee, the minority ranking member of the committee, and several other members of the committee, and I understand that the amendment is acceptable to them. I hope the chairman will take it to conference, and that it will be included in the final bill which Congress passes.[5]

The Republican majority accepted the amendment on unanimous consent. There were no hearings. There was no debate. The next day, the *Washington Post* explained the amendment to the country. It would, said the newspaper's editors, "withdraw tax-free status from any foundations or other organizations that attempt to 'influence legislation' or dabble in politics in behalf of any candidate for public office."[6]

Lyndon Johnson did not seem to have the matter of religion much in mind. He wanted to win an election. He wanted to stop the political use of tax-exempt organizations by his wealthy opponents. Yet his few minutes on the Senate floor in 1954 have meant that every tax-exempt church and ministry in America is kept from endorsing candidates or specific legislation if it wants to keep its tax-exempt status.

Of course, there are holes in the Johnson Amendment's wall of restraint. Political candidates commonly appear in like-minded churches or synagogues and the unspoken endorsement is assumed. Clergy speak in veiled terms about the morality of pending legislation and congregation members do not miss the point. Still, churches from both sides of the theological and political spectrum have lost their tax-exempt status for violating the IRS and the threat looms large to religious organizations nationwide.

America's clergy have become adept at working around the Johnson Amendment. Sometimes the results are quite humorous. When Al Gore and George W. Bush were battling for the presidency, Kenneth Edmonds of Jerusalem Full Baptist Church in Flint, Michigan, taught his congregation to kneel at bedtime and pray, "The Lord is my shepherd, I shall not vote for George Bush."[7] During this same election, the Reverend Jerry Falwell, preaching at the Genoa Baptist Church in Ohio, told worshipers to "vote for the Bush of your choice."[8] When Hillary Clinton ran for a New York Senate seat, she spoke at a Bronx church in which the pastor substituted the name of her opponent for Satan in the hymn of the day.[9]

None of this—the threat, the fear, or the humor—is lost on Donald Trump. Whatever his motives, he has made overturning the Johnson Amendment a priority for his administration and has even challenged leading clergy to hold him accountable for doing so. No other presidential candidate has been so outspoken about this law, a law which bedevils America's clergy as they seek to address the crises of the nation.

Trump's sense of urgency about abolishing this law has sometimes shocked even his closest advisors. During a conference call with his newly formed evangelical advisory council in 2016, the president-elect declared, "The only way I'm going to get to heaven is by repealing the Johnson Amendment." There was a pause. Many on the call were wondering about Trump's perception of what gets a man to heaven as well as his intense focus on repealing a law most Americans know nothing about.

Finally, someone spoke up and said, "No, sir. The only way you're going to get to heaven is by trusting Jesus Christ as your personal savior."

"Thank you for reminding me," Trump answered.[10]

However misaligned his religious priorities may be, Trump's devotion to repealing the Johnson Amendment is vital to one of the most unlikely acts of political repositioning in American electoral history. In the eyes of millions of Americans, Donald Trump has become a long-awaited champion of religious liberty, a man to undo the damage done by Barack Obama and to stem the tide of secularism flowing down from previous decades. This image has won Trump the devotion of America's most outspoken religious leaders and will serve to shape the priorities of his presidency as long as he remains in power.

Donald Trump is a fighter, and in the matter of the Johnson Amendment, he chose his fight well. It has won him widespread political support, and from sources he might never have otherwise engaged.

Yet he should be careful. Abolishing the Johnson Amendment may prove a double-edged sword. It will not only free conservative clergy to speak openly about politics but will free all clergy in the United States to take political stands and endorse candidates if they choose. Most of these are not the kind of clergy who would endorse Donald Trump. They are more left-leaning and will become champions for the other side. Trump may be dealing both himself—if and when he runs for a second term—and other conservatives a difficult hand to play.

There is also the matter that most Americans not only do not understand what the Johnson Amendment is but may not wish it abolished once they do understand it. Its central prohibition—that clergy and nonprofit organizations may not endorse political candidates—is likely a prohibition many Americans would prefer to keep in place. They are not likely to want their ministers to be more politically active, since there is some indication that most religious Americans believe their faith leaders are too political as it is.

Sounding the battle cry against the Johnson Amendment worked well for Trump during his campaign for president. Fashioning a livable peace after that battle—should he be successful—will be a far more daunting challenge.

8 | Obama

It is well-known that I am not fond of President Obama. I think he has been an awful president. His inexperience and arrogance have been very costly to this country. He's weakened our military, alienated our allies, and emboldened our enemies. He's abused his power by taking executive actions that he had no right to take. The next president is going to have to reverse and repeal many of the actions he's taken.

Donald Trump[1]

There was a time in American history when voters looked only for character and wisdom in their political candidates. Was there evidence of statesmanship? Was there the moral heft that befit high office? Were the marks of providence in view?

This changed over time. After the Watergate scandal of the early 1970s, something else moved to the fore. Americans hoped for essential goodness in answer to the secretive and snarling ways of Richard Nixon. Did candidates have a functioning moral compass? Could they be trusted to put the mechanisms of state only to noble use?

In the presidential election of 2016, there was a new standard by which Americans judged their candidates. It was the anger standard.

Who best gave voice to our political rage? Who best channeled the anger that kept us up at night? Who was the standard-bearer of our wrath?

By the time Donald Trump announced his candidacy for president, American political rage had reached flood stage. This does much to explain the Trump phenomenon, particularly his appeal to religious conservatives. For this tribe, the eight years of Barack Obama's presidency had been a time of unrelenting war on religion. No longer were religious conservatives regarded as the torchbearers of the nation's founding faith, they believed. Instead, they felt themselves the enemies of a goose-stepping progressive agenda.

Barack Obama was the reason for it all.

This is likely to be one of the enduring conundrums of the Obama presidency. It is especially disturbing given that Barack Obama is himself a Christian, the nearly one-quarter of Americans who at one time believed him a Muslim notwithstanding. He has repeatedly stated his belief in the core of the Christian gospel: that Jesus Christ is the Son of God, that he was crucified for the sins of humankind, that he was raised from the dead, and that he now rules the world at the right hand of God.

Obama affirmed these truths often during his presidency. He annually gave Easter talks on the meaning of Jesus that were so tender that they moved some White House staffers to tears. He enjoyed the preaching of an exceptionally fiery Southern Baptist Navy chaplain at Camp David. When a member of his team of spiritual advisors, evangelical pastor Dr. Joel Hunter, lost a grandchild to cancer, Obama quoted Scripture and the words of hymns to comfort the grieving grandfather. Hunter later said he would never forget how a president encouraged a pastor in distinctly Christian terms. Obama daily read a devotional written by his spiritual advisors, defended policy positions with Scripture, and was not beyond praying on his knees with fellow believers.

He could also move audiences with surprising glimpses into his spiritual life, as he did at the 2011 National Prayer Breakfast.

> When I wake in the morning, I wait on the Lord, and I ask Him to give me the strength to do right by our country and its people. And when I go to bed at night I wait on the Lord, and I ask Him to forgive me my sins, and look after my family and the American people, and make me an instrument of His will.
>
> I say these prayers hoping they will be answered, and I say these prayers knowing that I must work and must sacrifice and must serve to see them answered. But I also say these prayers knowing that the act of prayer itself is a source of strength. It's a reminder that our time on Earth is not just about us; that when we open ourselves to the possibility that God might have a larger purpose for our lives, there's a chance that somehow, in ways that we may never fully know, God will use us well.[2]

He was, then, a man shaped by the core truths of the Christian faith. He was a man who understood himself as having a God-ordained role to play. He was a president who understood his nation as having a divine obligation to fulfill.

Yet he was also a product of the most left-leaning Christian denomination on earth. By the time he entered the presidency, he had known only the preaching of the angry and unorthodox Rev. Jeremiah Wright and had been a member only of Chicago's Trinity United Church of Christ. This meant that Obama was shaped by a denomination so liberal that its clergy were not required to believe in the divinity of Jesus or the resurrection of the dead. It had ordained its first gay clergyman as early as 1972. The United Church of Christ had long aligned itself on the far left side of every political issue of relevance in the United States. This was the spiritual home of Barack Obama for the twenty years before he entered the Oval Office.

It was no surprise to his critics, then, that in an unguarded moment during the 2008 campaign, Obama described working-class white voters as people who "get bitter" and "cling to guns or religion, or antipathy to people who aren't like them. . . . as a way to explain their frustrations."[3] It is the thinking of a secular academic. Religion is neither revealed nor true. It is a product of the human mind, of social conditions. It is merely a psychological defense against the pain of life. Nothing more.

Was this the voice of the real Barack Obama? Was all else religious decoration designed to impress voters? Was this the reason he would agree to speak at a National Day of Prayer and end up chastising Christians in the audience for the sins of the Crusades? Was this why he went about declaring that America was no longer a Christian nation? Perhaps this explained his fixation on apologizing for his faith—particularly before Muslim audiences—rather than declaring its truth.

In the eyes of religious conservatives, then, Barack Obama was a man in conflict with himself. He was a religious Dr. Jekyll and Mr. Hyde, and the American people could never be sure which would emerge: the tender, Christian Obama or the anti-Christian leftist who with Freud, Marx, and Darwin believed religion was something humankind had created for itself and would be better off without.

Yet it was not just the tensions in Barack Obama's soul that inspired widespread anger. It was the way Obama led his administration in declaring war on Americans of faith.

He seemed, for example, to never have heard of an abortion he didn't like. As an Illinois state senator, he had gone so far as to support partial birth abortion, the practice of pulling a child partially from the womb before killing it. It was an affinity reflected in his Affordable Care Act, otherwise known as Obamacare. Despite the efforts of Republicans and pro-life Democrats, the mandates for abortion in the Act were so restrictive that it positioned the American government in opposition to a majority of the American people.

Catholics became targets. Their hospitals were threatened by the Obama administration for refusing to perform abortions. In one extreme case, the administration's lawyers descended on a small order of nuns called the Little Sisters of the Poor. Lawsuits were filed and appeals were made. The case ended up before the US Supreme Court, which in May 2016 vacated a lower court decision against the nuns.

Evangelicals were also targeted. Though the owners of the Hobby Lobby chain of stores provided exceptional medical care for their tens of thousands of employees, they were sued by their government because they refused to pay for abortion-inducing drugs as part of their company's insurance coverage. At one point, they faced fines of more than a million dollars a day. Through a series of appeals, they, too, ended up before the US Supreme Court. They, too, were vindicated.

Nevertheless, the Obama administration was seldom as certain on any issue as it was on abortion. Obama was the first US president to speak at a Planned Parenthood convention and was fiercely supportive when videos surfaced revealing that the organization had been illegally selling fetal tissue for profit. He vetoed a bill to defund Planned Parenthood in the wake of the scandal and intervened to stave off state-level defunding initiatives.

Gay rights also received full-throated support. Obama insisted that his attorney general, Eric Holder, cease defending the Defense of Marriage Act, which had been law in the United States since 1996. He also led the charge for the repeal of "Don't Ask/Don't Tell," allowing open homosexuality in America's armed forces. He reversed himself on same-sex marriage and celebrated the Supreme Court's *Obergefell v. Hodges* decision legalizing the practice. Few Americans will forget the night Mr. Obama ordered the White House lit up in the colors of the rainbow flag, symbol of the gay pride movement.

His administration never seemed as energized as it was by the concerns of lesbians, gays, bisexuals, or transgender Americans. He supported the prosecution of a bakery whose owners refused to make cakes for a gay wedding. He intervened in state-level deliberations about transgender use of restrooms. He supported the use of Medicare and Medicaid funds to pay for "gender reassignment surgery." To press his point further, he appointed a transgender man to a council of clergy. He issued an executive order barring federal contractors from discriminating on the basis of sexual orientation or gender identity and would not allow exemptions for religious organizations. Among his last acts in office was commuting the sentence of a transgender woman who leaked military secrets. Americans of faith took note. Under Barack Obama, their government had become an enemy of traditional faith, traditional values, and the tradition of limited government.

These Americans also took note when Secretary of State Hillary Clinton, speaking for the administration, declared before a watching world that "Lesbian, Gay, Bisexual, and Transgender rights" are "a priority of our foreign policy."[4] Most Americans were surprised to learn that in an age of terrorism and advancing tyranny, sexual matters had somehow moved forefront in US foreign policy. Where had the turn occurred? How had it become the business of the US government to force sexual behavior upon other countries? In fact, how had it become the business of the US government to force sexual behavior on its own citizens?

The administration was often so extreme in these matters that other nations began pushing back. In Kenya, a council of Islamic clergy and Christian ministers responded to US pressure on sexual ethics by declaring, "Simply because he has risen to be the President of a superpower does not mean he can now start acting as God."[5] The Vatican complained that the US government was becoming "progressively more hostile to Christian civilization."[6]

By the time of the 2016 presidential election, religious conservatives were angry and desperate for change. They didn't want a candidate who merely understood. They wanted a candidate who was as fierce and as angry as they were. They wanted someone bold and hard-hitting, even offensive. They felt their nation slipping away. They felt the ways of their fathers being lost.

Then came Donald Trump. He channeled their anger. He cut into their enemies. He promised to make their lives better and restore what had been lost.

They had never envisioned a man like him but they would take him, flaws and all, if he would help them take their nation back. In turn, they helped him win the White House and celebrated his victory as the end of the Obama administration's religious bombardment.

They took a risk. Their children were watching. The rest of America was watching. Whatever the Trump administration becomes, they will be required to reconcile it with what they say they believe about God and his truth.

Their anger, justified or not, won the day. Now, though, they are wed to Donald Trump before a watching world.

9 Hillary

Such a nasty woman.

Donald Trump[1]

There will long be debate about the election that put Donald Trump in the White House. How did a controversial real estate mogul with no political experience defeat a slate of experienced Republicans in the primaries and then achieve victory over a Democratic heir-apparent who was also one of the most seasoned politicians in the country? A century from now, professors will still be probing the minutiae of the 2016 presidential race before classrooms of astonished students.

There will be much to explore. Did Hillary Clinton's primary battle with Bernie Sanders exhaust her campaign? What damage was done when she called half of Donald Trump's supporters a "basket of deplorables"?[2] How was it possible that Clinton could raise $242 million more than Trump, outgun him three to one in television ads, receive 2.8 million more popular votes than he did, and yet still lose? Why did her campaign wait until October 29 to run a television ad in Wisconsin, a state she lost by just twenty-two thousand votes ten days later? The questions will likely never end.

The topic of religion will certainly inspire some of these questions. Though Hillary Clinton possessed a deeper religious history and wider religious knowledge, and was more articulate in expressing her faith than her opponent, she failed to capitalize on any of these advantages. Instead, her campaign was marked by a surprising neglect of religious voters. This was odd for a candidate who held her first campaign rally at New York's Four Freedoms Park, named for Franklin Roosevelt's famous 1941 speech celebrating freedom of speech, freedom of worship, freedom from want, and freedom from fear. Not only in her speech at the New York rally but also throughout her campaign, Clinton never managed to mention the matter of worship.

It was a shocking omission, particularly since Donald Trump had given clear warning he planned to use religion against her. This occurred as early as June 2016, when Trump spoke to a gathering of evangelicals on the sixth floor of the Marriott Marquis in Times Square. "We don't know anything about Hillary in terms of religion," Trump declared. "Now, she's been in the public eye for years and years, and yet there's nothing out there. It's going to be an extension of Obama but it's going to be worse, because with Obama you had your guard up. With Hillary, you don't, and it's going to be worse."[3]

Though little of this was true, it was a shot across the Clinton campaign's bow that ought to have been noticed. It ought to have brought faith to the fore in the campaign's messaging. It didn't. Instead, the opposite occurred.

Clinton did mention her Methodist faith in her convention acceptance speech and did appear at a handful of African-American churches during her campaign. Apart from this, the campaign's treatment of Clinton's faith was virtually nonexistent. Directors of faith outreach were appointed far too late in the game. Religious media were denied access. The campaign never did respond to requests by leading evangelical magazine *Christianity Today* for an interview. The all-important matter of symbolism was mismanaged as well. Clinton's first speech after receiving her party's nomination for the presidency took place at a Planned Parenthood event. This was guaranteed to distance religious conservatives, many of whom were uncertain about Trump and a portion of whom might have responded to a lean in their direction by Clinton. It never occurred.

Yet there is a broader issue than simply campaign mismanagement in this matter of faith and Hillary Clinton. There is also the reality that she represents a murky, ever fluctuating, uncertain brand of left-leaning spirituality that many Americans find difficult to understand and just as many distrust. Little might have been said of this had she not throughout her life consistently put her faith at the forefront of her politics. Hillary Clinton is one of the most faith-based politicians of our generation. There has been time for Americans to know what can be known of her religious views. It hasn't happened. Though she has been on the national stage for more than a quarter of a century, at the start of the 2016 presidential campaign season, almost half of all Americans—some 43 percent—perceived Clinton as having no religion at all.[4]

The truth is far different from the popular perception. She grew up in a deeply Methodist family permeated by religion. "We talked with God, walked with God, ate, studied, and argued with God. Each night we knelt by our beds to pray," she wrote.[5] At the family's Park Ridge Methodist Church, she first heard the famous words of John Wesley that would come to define her life's purpose: "Do all the good you can, by all the means you can, in all the ways you can, at all the times you can, to all the people you can, as long as you ever can." A youth minister at Park Ridge schooled her both in the Bible and in the rising currents of the 1960s counterculture: the lyrics of Bob Dylan, the cadences of beat poet Jack Kerouac, and the speeches of Martin Luther King Jr.

It was a spiritual imprint that would remain with her through Wellesley, Yale Law School, marriage to Bill Clinton, and into her role as First Lady of Arkansas. She experienced the same ebbs and flows of spiritual passion and doubt that most people of faith do, but she retained what Park Ridge Methodist Church imparted to her soul. Her pastor in Little Rock later recalled, "One of her favorite thoughts was that the goal of life is to restore what has been lost, to find oneness with God, and until we find this we are lonely."[6]

It was when she became First Lady of the United States that she began experimenting with religion in a way that would shape her for decades after. She still held to the core Christian truths of her youth. In a much-cited interview, Bob Woodward pressed Clinton about whether she was still an "old-fashioned Methodist."

Woodward: "Do you believe in the Father, Son and Holy Spirit?"
First Lady: "Yes."
Woodward: "The atoning death of Jesus?"
First Lady: "Yes."
Woodward: "The resurrection of Christ?"
First Lady: "Yes."[7]

As orthodox as she could sound, she had also begun leaning to nontraditional religious influences. She hosted White House gatherings of leaders from nearly every alternative religious stream. She even famously consented to what amounted to a séance with noted spiritualist Jean Houston. Though news of it proved embarrassing, there was no clearer evidence that Hillary Clinton was in search of help to withstand her husband's betrayals, the bludgeoning of an unsympathetic press, and the stresses that any First Lady is forced to endure. She was in search of something to answer the needs of her soul. The truths of her Methodist upbringing were no longer enough.

She carried her religious ideals into the Senate, where she invoked her faith often. When Republicans proposed an offending immigration bill, she bashed them with biblical force. "It is certainly not in keeping with my understanding of the Scriptures," she scolded. "This bill would liberally criminalize the Good Samaritan—and probably even Jesus himself."[8] When John Kerry lost the presidency to George W. Bush, she mourned, "No one can read the New Testament of our Bible without recognizing that Jesus had a lot more to say about how we treat the poor than most of the issues that were talked about in this election."[9]

What was missing were understandable connections between her faith and her politics. If she was going to put her faith in play politically, she had an obligation to explain what the content of that faith was. She never did during her Senate years. This was vital, chiefly because she had chosen to move to the left edge of American politics. As one biographer has written, "Not a single US senator was more liberal on economic and social matters than Mrs. Clinton, and in 2003, no senator surpassed her liberal ranking on social issues."[10] Her unswerving pro-abortion politics tell the tale. The Christian Coalition and the National Right to Life Committee both put her at zero. Meanwhile, the National Abortion and Reproductive Rights Action League gave her a stunning 100 percent.[11]

To this move from centrist to extreme left she added a confusing abandonment of faith-based positions she had once championed. Though her husband had signed the Defense of Marriage Act (DOMA) into law and she had fiercely defended it with Scripture quotations at the time, she began moving in the opposite direction. This shift marked her years as secretary of state and her campaigns for president. She described the change as fruit of "the guiding principles of my faith" but offered no further explanation.[12]

She repudiated DOMA and rejoiced when President Obama instructed his Justice Department to stop defending it. She then began transforming herself into a champion of gay rights. No one publicly celebrated the Supreme Court's *Obergefell v. Hodges* decision legalizing same sex marriage more than Hillary Clinton.

Her advocacy for abortion knew no bounds. As late as 2007, she had shared her husband's commitment that abortion in America should be "safe, legal and rare." Soon after, she dropped the "rare." Unfettered abortion access became her litmus test for a just society. Nothing must stand in its way, even convictions of faith. At a global conference of women in New York, she declared that abortion rights required that "deep-seated cultural codes, religious beliefs and structural biases have to be changed."[13] She later insisted that a woman's decision to get an abortion is a decision "based on her faith" but she never explained what this meant.[14]

Nothing revealed her extreme support for abortion rights like the scandal that plagued Planned Parenthood in 2015. In that year, videos went viral that depicted Planned Parenthood officials illegally negotiating the sale of organs from fetal tissue. One described how a fetus can be "crushed" to preserve livers, lungs, and hearts "intact." Another joked that she wanted a Lamborghini for her services and then explained the "crunchy" procedures used to harvest fetal organs. Hillary Clinton defended it all.

By the time she ran for president against Donald Trump, she was the candidate most outspoken about having a faith and the least clear about the meaning of that faith. It was possible to wonder if her religion was nothing more than mystical justification for whatever she decided to do. Did it have any ethical content? Were there any firm lines? Was there a sense that God had spoken final truth to all humankind, or was her religion based on what Barack Obama called a "living word" that constantly morphed and evolved? It was impossible to know, for while faith was ever-present in Hillary Clinton's politics it was also ever ill-defined and unexplained.

The truth of this was confirmed by her race against Donald Trump. She certainly had the longer religious history. She was better-spoken in matters of faith. She ought to have bested Trump at every religious turn.

He was, after all, the man who claimed faith but said he had never found reason to ask forgiveness of God. He was the candidate who eagerly held up a Bible his grandmother had given him and then excitedly told a national television audience that she had even written his address in it. When asked about the role of God in his life, he spoke of his many victories in business. When asked about God's role in the nation, he confirmed that the United States is the greatest country in the world. Reporters sought religious depth or even basic understanding in vain.

Yet Hillary Clinton lost ground with religious voters when compared with the previous Democratic standard-bearer, Barack Obama. He had won support from 26 percent of evangelicals in 2008 and 20 percent in 2012. She drew only 16 percent in 2016. Meanwhile, Donald Trump drew an astonishing 81 percent, more than George W. Bush, John McCain, or Mitt Romney in their presidential runs.

It was a stunning feat, and it was only possible because by the 2016 presidential race a large portion of voters were weary of politicians touting religion without dimension, religion that was ever invoked but seldom defined. They preferred someone like them—raw, imperfect, but fierce in defense of what they believed. This left them only one choice: Donald Trump.

10 | Voice

> I think people are tired of politically correct people, where ev-
> erything comes out "The sun will rise and be beautiful." I think
> people are really tired of politically correct.
>
> Donald Trump[1]

On Thursday, July 21, 2016, Donald Trump accepted the Republican Party nomination for president of the United States. He
did so in a sometimes rambling, sometimes stirring speech that
lasted an hour and fifteen minutes. It was the longest party nomination acceptance speech in American history.

It had all the expected fire and bluster. It even included some un-
characteristic humility. In a reference to his support among religious
conservatives, Trump wondered aloud if he was worthy. "I would
like to thank the evangelical community," he said, "because, I will
tell you what, the support they have given me—and I'm not sure I
totally deserve it—has been so amazing."[2]

Yet in the more than five thousand words of the speech, there
were four that captured a truth that may be at the heart of Trump's
improbable climb to the White House. They were the words, "I am
your voice."

He was speaking of the "ignored, neglected, and abandoned" when he said these words. He had evoked "laid-off factory workers" and "communities crushed by our horrible and unfair trade deals." He summoned to mind "forgotten men and women of our country" who "no longer have a voice."

"I am your voice," he then promised.

He meant, of course, that he would be a champion for the economically oppressed, yet these four words are more far-reaching than he may have intended. The truth is that much of the appeal of Donald Trump is the way he speaks publicly in the same way that millions of Americans do around kitchen tables, at bars, and among their closest friends. Crass, insulting, bullying, sometimes ill-informed, always opinionated, usually prejudiced, Donald Trump is very much the private voice of millions of Americans. This is one of the main reasons for his rise to the presidency.

It is an oddity that scholars will long debate. Throughout his life, Donald Trump breathed only rarified air. He knew great wealth from birth and as an adult was numbered among the global elite. Yet he mastered a common touch. He could comment to reporters with the manner of a New York dockworker before slipping into his limousine with his supermodel wife and returning to the fifty-eight-story Manhattan building that was his home. When he did, street vendors and corner cops cheered him. They heard themselves in him, in his matter-of-fact arrogance and his mafioso-like tone of threat. He was "the people's billionaire."

It is the familiarity of his voice that wins him affection far beyond his class and kind. One biographer believes that when the average American listens to Trump, "The way he talks reminds them of the voice inside their own heads—a rich and sometimes dark stew of conversational snippets and memory scraps, random phrases and half-thoughts—and by extension, it somehow seems as if they're hearing the voice inside his head."[3]

Trump is not unlike, then, a guilty pleasure. People often speak in private in ways they would be ashamed to speak in public. They have their bigotries. They have their conceits. They have their stumbling, yet-unformed thoughts that they fully intend to repeat as often as it pleases them. They cite facts they've been told aren't true, but they like the sound of their voice in the retelling and they do not plan to edit themselves anytime soon. Punctuate it all with cussing and the almost meaningless phrases used for emphasis—"Trust me" and "I'm tellin' ya"—and it all forms into the public speech of Donald Trump. It is a scandal to American media and a call to arms for his political opponents.

"But to his supporters," contends Gwenda Blair, Trump's biographer, "it is proof that he is the real deal—not focus grouped, not mediated, not hiding behind a mask of calculation and manipulation. They admire and, in some cases, envy Trump for openly expressing a deepest self that seems to mirror what they think and feel but don't dare reveal to the world."[4] He is, in brief, refreshing, especially in the wake of the always polished, ever even-toned, never-far-from-a-teleprompter Barack Obama.

What this leads to is a conclusion that horrifies those wearing "Not My President" T-shirts and hoping for impeachment any minute. Donald Trump is not a right-wing alien who has invaded American politics. He is, instead, very typical of what America has become. He is an exemplar, a representation. As Trump biographer Michael D'Antonio has written, "Donald Trump is not a man apart. He is, instead, merely one of us writ large."[5]

This will not sit well with members of the media or Trump's political opponents who prefer to portray him as a barbarian who made it through the gates. He is, instead, a vocal member of the barbarian nation within those gates. Indeed, it could be that, politics aside, what is most significant about Trump is what he reveals of America in the second decade of the twenty-first century.

He has, for example, used foul language in his public speeches more than any presidential candidate or president in recent memory—perhaps worse than in the whole of American history. As fashionable as it is to express offense at his crass, profanity-laden way of talking, Trump is merely typical of his times. Some 74 percent of Americans report hearing profanity regularly and 64 percent admit they use strong language themselves. Two thirds of Americans believe people swear more than they did twenty years ago.[6] We live in an age when television commercials, Sunday sermons in church, and even blogs about cooking are likely to include language that not long ago was considered foul. Trump has not tainted American culture by his crass talk. He has merely reflected it.

He has been married three times and has boasted publicly of his infidelity to his wives. This is mentioned often in media reports. Yet, again, it is a behavior in keeping with trends in American society. Between 30 and 60 percent of all married individuals will engage in infidelity at some point during their marriages. The number of men and women who admit to having affairs with co-workers is 36 percent. When women wonder if their partners are having affairs, 85 percent of them are proven right. When men wonder the same, 50 percent are right. Trump is merely a product of his times.[7]

It is the same with church attendance. Donald Trump wants to be seen as a Christian yet admits to rarely attending church in recent decades. In this, he is at home in American culture. According to the Hartford Institute of Religion Research, while more than 40 percent of Americans say they go to church weekly, only 20 percent of Americans actually do. Some 2.7 million church members fall into inactivity each year. Between 2010 and 2012, half of all US churches did not add any new members. Clearly, fewer Americans are going to church than ever in American history. Donald Trump has joined them.[8]

He is often accused of misrepresenting facts or outright lying on a regular basis. Perhaps it is true. Yet, if so, he is merely keeping pace with most Americans. A University of Massachusetts study reveals that 60 percent of adults can't have a ten-minute conversation without lying at least once.[9] Americans lie the most to their parents (86 percent), their friends (75 percent), their siblings (73 percent), and their spouses (69 percent).[10]

Some of Trump's public statements have been tinged with racial bigotry. It is offensive and inexcusable. It is also a prominent feature of American society. Racial bias appears in nearly every arena of American life. One study reveals that though marijuana use is roughly equal among whites and blacks, blacks are four times more likely than whites to be arrested for the practice.[11] An ESPN fan survey reported that black fans esteemed African-American athletes far more highly than white fans. LeBron James was viewed positively by 57 percent of blacks but just 24 percent of whites. Tiger Woods was adored by 48 percent of blacks but only 19 percent of whites. Only Michael Jordan transcended race and was esteemed by both whites and blacks.[12] Once again, Donald Trump is a product of his time and his nation's culture.

None of this is a defense of Trump. Instead, it raises searing questions for those who supported him, pro-Trump clergy in particular. To support Donald Trump without caveat, to extol him as chosen by God without identifying what is morally objectionable in his politics and behavior, is much the same as extolling American culture without expressing any moral reservation.

Donald Trump is merely a man. He cannot be held responsible for the immoral drift of American society. Yet for those who are the guardians of morality and whose role it is to call for stronger character and deeper souls, to support Trump publicly without distinguishing between the virtues and the vices is nearly an act of idolatry.

When Trump declared at the 2016 GOP convention, "I am your voice," he meant it mainly in an economic sense. Yet he may have inadvertently stated a broader truth. He is a supercharged version of what America has become. He is the average American today written large. Perhaps he is even a cultural GPS for our times.

He once said, "I am the American Dream, supersized version." Perhaps, once again, he was saying more than he knew.[13]

PART 4

Of Prophets and Presidents

Donald Trump is an undisciplined man of unguarded tongue, ill-focused mind, and turbulent soul. He has been ruled most of his life by rage and the will to win, by the animal forces competition surfaces in him. Yet he is surrounded by some of the most celebrated religious leaders in the nation. Among the best hopes for the Trump presidency is that these religious conservatives do what they did not do during his campaign for office: speak the truth of faith to their president and find the courage to spur him on to being a better man than he has ever been before.

11 The Art of Prophetic Distance, Part I

T he presidency is not the papacy. Most Roman Catholics believe that when a pope is chosen, the man is changed by his ordination, transformed by the Holy Spirit into more than he has ever been. Americans do not have the same expectation of their presidents. They do not believe that the taking of the presidential oath does anything to change the nature of the person. They will be what they have always been. In fact, they are likely to be more of what they have been once they take office. This is why elections are often backward-looking affairs. We do not know the future and are just experiencing the present. The only way we can know if a man or a woman is qualified for the Oval Office is to look to their past.

When it comes to Donald Trump, this can be a disturbing experience. Whatever his gifts, he is a deeply imperfect man who has lived his life on a large scale. His deformities are obvious. The oddities of his personality frequently appear.

There is, for example, the now-famous episode of the speech he gave at his father's funeral. Fred Trump, Donald's father, died on June 25, 1999. The funeral was four days later. The 650 guests were treated to speeches by Reverend Arthur Caliandro, Norman Vincent Peale's successor at the church, and by Rudolph Giuliani, mayor of New York. Then the Trump children spoke. Robert Trump said his father was his hero. Maryanne Trump, a federal judge, read a letter she had written to her father during her college days. Others spoke lovingly and movingly of the man.

When it was Donald's turn, the topic was not what his father meant to him but rather what he meant to his father. He explained that he had heard of his father's death after just reading a story in the *New York Times* extolling the success of one of his real estate projects, Trump Place. It reminded him that his father had always believed in him, that on this project as with the Grand Hyatt, Trump Tower, Trump Plaza, the Trump Taj Mahal, and Trump Castle, his father had known he would win and would always be a success.

On display was the familiar Donald Trump stronghold of self. Even at his own father's funeral, he could not keep from promoting himself, from affirming himself—perhaps as a substitute for Fred Trump's lack of affirmation. Yet that it was done publicly, unashamedly, before a solemn crowd and a grieving family, seemed brazen, even callous. This was the Donald Trump the world was beginning to know.

There are dozens of such stories from Donald Trump's life, moments when he seems an unabashed force of self, incapable of viewing the world apart from his central role in it. This tells us much that we need to know. Whatever good he might bring to his presidency, he will also bring the soul of a successful man wrapped around the neediness of an unwisely fathered boy. It will make him haughty, pretentious, self-affirming, and often vicious when challenged.

He will need moral guardians around him, then. He will need the pastors and clergy and ministers of truth he so esteems. He does not keep friends for long and is not open to input from those he does not know and trust. He has an unusual regard, though, for those he perceives to speak for God, and these will need to be bolder and more pointed than they ever were during his campaign.

It is not an easy role to assume, either in the life of Donald Trump or that of any other president. Events move by at dizzying speeds, and presidents have many voices ringing in their ears. It is easy for religious leaders to play a ceremonial role but much harder to be heard at a meaningful depth, to a degree that penetrates the heart of the nation's leader and does any lasting good. An example is surely found in the public life of Billy Graham, a revered religious leader who worked to speak truth to power but found it difficult and sometimes humiliating. One of his first attempts in particular was an agonizing failure.

In 1950, when Graham was just gaining fame for his huge evangelistic crusades, he asked for an opportunity to visit with President Harry Truman. The meeting was arranged, the two men discussed the cause of the Christian gospel in America, and then Graham said a brief prayer. That should have been the end of it: a successful moment with a sitting president.

Then Graham's naiveté came into play. When he walked out of the White House, he was quickly besieged by newspaper reporters and photographers. They, of course, asked what had happened in the Oval Office. What had he and the president said? When Graham mentioned the time in prayer, the reporters asked him to reenact it. They knew what sport they could make of a young preacher acting out an Oval Office prayer on the front lawn of the White House. Graham, of course, had no idea he was being set up. Unwisely, he knelt and repeated the prayer, all for the encircling cameras.

The photos adorned the front pages of the nation's leading newspapers the next day. Graham looked like a fool. Truman was incensed. The preacher apologized and did not forget for the rest of his days how easy it was to make such excruciating mistakes.

It might have been worse. Though Graham could not have known it, politicians would soon begin thinking of him not mainly as a spiritual leader but as a man who could enhance their political power. Several years after Graham met with Truman, he also met with Dwight Eisenhower. Afterward, the hero/general who was then president wrote a friend:

> Billy Graham came to see me. . . . I quite agree with you regarding his remarkable ability to reach millions of our people with a spiritual message. . . . Since all pastors must necessarily take a nonpartisan approach, it would be difficult to form any formal organization of religious leaders to work on our behalf. However, this might be done in an informal way.[1]

These words are a behind-the-scenes look at how the political often views the religious. Graham was at that time an eager young evangelist hoping to help return America to the God of her founding era. He wrote letters informing Eisenhower of the progress of his crusades and assuring the aged president, "People are hungry for God."[2] Whatever regard Eisenhower may have had for Graham's religious work, he saw the preacher mainly as a man who commanded a large audience and who might be convinced to serve political ends.

It was a recurrent theme in Graham's life and was particularly evident in his relationship with Richard Nixon. The two men were friends, met often, and frequently discussed spiritual matters. Yet when the Watergate tapes became public and Nixon could be heard in an unrehearsed state, Graham was faced with the foul language, racism, duplicity, and vindictiveness that marked the Nixon presidency.

In 1997, Graham reflected upon how he might have been deceived. "Looking back these forty-five years later, considering all that has intervened, I wonder whether I might have exaggerated his spirituality in my own mind." His next sentence is reminiscent of moments in Donald Trump's 2016 campaign. "But then, in my presence, he always made ready references to his mother's faith and the Bible that she loved so much." Graham's conclusion? "Where religion was concerned with him, it was not always easy to tell the difference between the spiritual and the sentimental. In retrospect, whenever he spoke about the Lord, it was in pretty general terms."[3]

Graham knew he had been seduced. This was plainly evident in a 1972 conversation he had with Nixon that was recorded by the now infamous White House taping system. Drawn in by Nixon's deep-seated anti-Semitism, Graham said, "A lot of the Jews are great friends of mine. They swarm around me and are friendly to me because they know that I'm friendly with Israel. But they don't know how I really feel about what they are doing to this country."[4]

He became a friend to presidents largely to fulfill the mandate of his ministry, as part of preaching his gospel to America and the world. Yet as the years went by, he realized he had often been manipulated by politicians with their eye only on power rather than God, and perhaps also by his own ambitions and gullibility. This gave him perspective on the Religious Right that arose near the end of his public life. Rather than celebrate it as might be expected, Graham was concerned that religious leaders who sought political influence might easily become tools of politics alone apart from any religious purpose. "It would disturb me if there was a wedding between the religious fundamentalists and the political right," he told *Parade* magazine in 1981. "The hard right has no interest in religion except to manipulate it."[5]

Graham's conclusion about his own ministry was telling. After all of his years of friendships with presidents and being asked to comment on politics, he finally realized, "I have one message"—the gospel.[6] He decided in his later years that he could have done more good by speaking his truth to presidents and politicians than by allowing himself to be pulled into their orbits, thus dissipating his message.

It is a lesson that even today would benefit the movement founded by Jerry Falwell. As the nation approached its bicentennial, religious leaders were disappointed with what they saw in American culture.

The renewed emphasis on the intentions of the founding fathers that accompanied the nation's two hundredth anniversary also re-introduced religious leaders to the founders' intentions for church and state. As Falwell expressed:

> Somehow I thought the separation doctrine existed to keep the church out of politics. I was wrong. In fact, to our nation's forefathers, especially Thomas Jefferson and his colleagues from our state of Virginia, the separation of church and state had been designed to keep the government from interfering with the church. Never during the founding years of this great democracy had our forefathers meant to distance the government from the truths of the Christian faith or to prohibit Christians from applying biblical principles in their influence on the state.[7]

While some historians would argue with Falwell's interpretation of the meaning of the First Amendment, most would accept Falwell's broader case: the founders had no intention of banning voices of faith from the public square. Over time, though, the problem in Falwell's day became what those voices of faith espoused, and this brings us closer to the issue of religion's role in the Trump administration.

During the decades from the Reagan presidency to the beginning of the Trump years, the religious right was often more politically right than genuinely religious, more conservative and even libertarian than biblical in its message. This was largely due to some of the very factors that led to a resurgence of conservative ideas.

Literature played a primary role. In the latter half of the twentieth century, there was a renaissance of conservative political writing that both challenged the prevailing liberalism and fed a growing movement. This began with William Buckley, founder of *National Review*, whose groundbreaking book *God and Man at Yale* challenged secular orthodoxy and called for an approach to politics informed by faith and tradition. He said it was the task of conservatism to stand athwart the course of history and shout, "Stop!"

Other writers stood with him. Among the most influential were libertarian economist Milton Friedman, free enterprise champion George Gilder, political scientist Charles Murray, syndicated African-American social theorist Thomas Sowell, African-American libertarian scholar Walter E. Williams, and eminent historian, social theorist, and fiction writer Russell Kirk. These sired hundreds more, leading to modern conservative voices such as Ann Coulter, Rush Limbaugh, Glenn Beck, Jonah Goldberg, Victor Hanson, Mark Steyn, John Stossel, and the revered Charles Krauthammer.

As valuable as the contributions of these and other conservative writers were, as much as they provided an antidote to the statism, secularism, and creeping socialism of the age, their ideas did not capture the essence of a biblical view of society. Nor was this their task. Yet when conservative religious leaders made secular conservatism the sum of their thinking about American society, they fell short of the best that a biblical worldview had to offer. This, in turn, often made them little more than a minor part of the proverbial "Republican party at prayer."

Conservative thinking may have claimed, for example, that government wasn't the solution but rather the problem, but religious leaders declaring the Bible as the basis of their politics were bound to believe that governments were ordained by God and derived authority from him.

Some conservative voices may have come close to insisting that poverty was in nearly all cases a result of laziness, addiction, or poor genetics, but the Scriptures that gave religious conservatives their reason for existence taught that poverty can also be the result of oppression, unjust laws, manipulation of the free market, and abuse of the laborer.

Economic conservatives might exalt the rich as the risk-takers and investors who made a nation prosperous, but the Bible pointed to an alternative view: "Do not pervert justice; do not show partiality to the poor or favoritism to the great, but judge your neighbor fairly."[8]

Neoconservatives might extol American democracy and insist that it was their role to construct similar democracies around the world, but biblically informed religious leaders had to recognize that there is no single, prescribed form of national government taught in the pages of the Bible.

Thus, many conservative ideas were helpful, corrective, and true— but they were not necessarily the best counsel of the Christian faith. The result was, then, that conservative religious leaders who did not hold Scripture above secular conservatism did not provide the alternative counsel they should have. They ought to have offered a third way that stood apart from liberalism and conservatism. They ought to have been voices from another realm. They ought to have been more than echoes and done more than merely sanction a secular conservative consensus.

Recovering this "third way" is particularly urgent for those who will have opportunity to influence Donald Trump. Consider what this might mean, for example, when it comes to the all-important issue of race. Trump has made at least racially inappropriate if not outright racist statements on many an occasion. Conservative religious leaders have largely stood by silently as he did. Yet these clergy make much of following the example of Jesus Christ, who went to great lengths to demonstrate his opposition to racial bigotry.

Consider what the meaning of a single episode from the life of Jesus might mean for the Trump administration and for the nation as a whole. Among the most shocking scenes that come down to us from the life of Jesus Christ was his violent explosion of anger in the Jewish temple of his day. This happened twice, once at the start of his public life and once just before his death. We are told that he erupted upon entering the temple courts. He began yelling and flipping over tables. He made a whip of reeds and threatened workers if they continued carrying goods along their usual route.

Why the commotion? Many readers simply conclude that Jesus was upset that business was being done in a holy place. This is suggested by the words Jesus spoke as he drove merchants from the temple courts: "My house will be a house of prayer, but you have made it 'a den of robbers.'"[9]

Yet the reason Jesus became angry was that the merchants had set up their trade in the only place the Gentiles had to pray—the Court of Gentiles. In fact, the words of Jesus—"my house will be a house of prayer"—were taken from the prophet Isaiah. Some of the Gospels do not cite the entire quote. It says in full, "my house will be called a house of prayer *for all nations*."[10] Jesus was not rebuking people for conducting business. He was rebuking them for callous, racist hearts.

The conclusion, then, is that the angriest, most riotous moment in the earthly life of Jesus Christ was due to the offense of racism. Heartless merchants had set up their trade in the only place the Gentiles—the "unclean ones" of the day—were allowed to pray. This is what incensed Jesus. This is why he raged, and not once but twice in his public life.

In an America battling new waves of racial tension, what might come from a bold, unapologetic declaration of the meaning of this episode in the life of Christ—that racism is sin, that it is un-Christian, and that any president who claims to be a follower of Christ must fight this evil with every weapon possible?

This is what is required of ministers who step into the lives of presidents. They are not there merely to affirm. They are not there simply to sanction. They are there to confront and speak truth that brings change. They are there to maintain prophetic distance and to be guardians of a moral vision for life and government.

12 | The Art of Prophetic Distance, Part II

There is an almost humorous tale of kings and prophets that comes down to us from the ancient world. It seems that two kings met millennia ago to discuss plans for going to war against a common enemy. In the manner of that time, they were eager to consult prophets and seers before finalizing their plans. One of the kings, then, trotted out four hundred wise men and diviners, all of whom said the same thing: *Go. You will be victorious. All is well.*

The other king knew something was wrong. The four hundred were obviously paid lackeys who gave whatever advice they thought their king wanted to hear. The doubtful king asked, "Is there no true prophet here of whom we can inquire?" He had heard from the sycophants. He wanted to hear a genuine voice.

The king who had produced the four hundred replied, "There is still one prophet through whom we can inquire, but I hate him because he never prophesies anything good about me, but always bad."

Ah. Finally. The truth. Still, the kings needed guidance, so they sent a messenger to retrieve the dreaded prophet. When the messenger found the man, he said, "Look, the other prophets without exception are predicting success for the king. Let your word agree with theirs, and speak favorably."

This was the way it had always been done. Tell a king what he wanted to hear and all would be fine. Agree with his other wise men and you might rise. It was the way to live long and prosper.

Yet it wasn't the way the prophet in question conducted himself. His name was Micaiah, and he told the king's messenger firmly what he would have to do: "I can only say what I know to be true."

This was not good news to the messenger. Still, he took his contentious prophet back to the two kings who were eagerly waiting. The king who had endured much abuse from Micaiah was especially impatient. "Shall we go to war . . . or not?"

"Attack and be victorious," the stubborn prophet replied, "for victory will be delivered into your hand."

They were the words the kings wanted to hear but they also detected a certain tone in the prophet's voice. He was mocking them. He was telling them what they wanted to hear in a tone that said none of it was true.

The offended king, furious now, said, "How many times must I make you swear to tell me nothing but the truth?"

This moved the prophet to speak: "I saw all your armies scattered on the hills like sheep without a shepherd."

"Didn't I tell you?" said the disgusted king. "He never says anything good about me."

And so it continued. In time, a battle was fought. One of the kings was killed. Troops were scattered. The four hundred prophets were proven false. Only Micaiah, who spoke the truth but was not heard, was proven true. "I hate him," the king had said, "because he never prophesies anything good about me."[1]

The story of Micaiah prompts a smile when we read it. Clergy teaching from it in churches and synagogues usually have great fun in the retelling. There is a seriousness in it, though. It reminds us that those who speak religious truth must stand apart. They must maintain prophetic distance. They must separate themselves to a degree from the powerful and from the people—from anything that might seduce them or taint their message—so that they can speak clearly and truthfully what they have been given to say. To do otherwise would be to compromise both the message and the call.

It is in the nature of rulers to seek counsel. It is in the nature of those burdened with great authority and far-reaching decisions to want to know what the gods or the fates or the auguries or the heavens portend. This is the reason ancient kings kept vast companies of wise men and seers. It is also why kings and queens keep chaplains at court even to this day.

In American history, this has usually taken the form of a president seeking input from a member of the clergy. We should be glad of this in most cases. Clergy have counseled presidents personally, advised on national policy, and reminded them of priorities drawn from sacred texts and natural law. Sometimes they have even kept presidents from going over the edge.

One of the most touching of these episodes occurred during the presidency of Abraham Lincoln. Less than a year after moving into the White House, Lincoln lost his beloved son, Willie, to typhoid fever. The boy died horribly. Lincoln was devastated. It would have been a shattering experience for him had it been the first death Lincoln had known, but he was a man acquainted with grief. He watched his mother die a ghastly death of "milk sickness" when he was a child, lost his only sister when he was just sixteen, and lost the first romantic love of his life when he was in his early twenties. He often admitted to friends that he was haunted by the thought of rain falling on graves.

Though we do not read of it in our textbooks, Lincoln suffered from agonizing bouts of depression.[2] He came close to killing himself on more than one occasion. Those close to him feared it might be the same after the death of Willie. One day a week, Lincoln locked himself in a dark room to grieve. Friends wondered if there would be a day when he never came out.

It was then that Dr. Francis Vinton, an Episcopal priest from New York, made an appointment to see Lincoln. He did not intend to comfort the president. He intended to pull the man out of his spiral of grief. The nation was at war and needed its commander in chief.

Vinton greeted Lincoln and immediately told him why he had come. He was in the White House to tell the president that his grieving had become excessive, that it would prove unhealthy both to Lincoln and his family, and that it might even be sin. This was bold. Vinton was taking a risk. Still, he was certain of his purpose. He reminded the stricken president of the resurrection and assured him that he would see his son again one day.

"He is alive," Vinton concluded.

Lincoln, jumping from his seat, was in no mood to be toyed with. "Alive! *Alive!* Surely you mock me."

"No, sir, believe me," replied Dr. Vinton; "it is a most comforting doctrine of the church founded upon the words of Christ himself."

The meeting continued awhile longer. Vinton left material for Lincoln to read and then returned to New York. Whatever we might think of the priest's message and methods from our distance, Lincoln improved. He began to right himself, temper his grief, and, though wounded, return to the work of the nation.[3]

This story of a relatively obscure Episcopal priest reminds us of the good that courageous voices of faith can do. If they will set themselves to tell the truth, if they will remember that they are emissaries from another land, they can remind leaders—who are too often mired in the temporal—of higher purposes and surer boundaries. They have the power to fix vision upon the eternal. They can call to mind the needs of the poor. They can challenge greed and corruption. They can even help align priorities and spending in a manner that befits a great nation.

Yet they can do all this only if they are willing to stand apart, only if they are willing to maintain prophetic distance. They must wish nothing for themselves. They must be free of any selfish agenda. They must speak only as the dictates of their faith require. They must do this both as they speak to the powerful and as they speak to the people of their land.

In the 2016 presidential race, the art of prophetic distance seemed lost to all but a few of the nation's clergy. So heated was the election and so great were the issues at stake that men and women of the cloth seemed to forget themselves. Many left their loftier roles as spokespersons for God and became agents of the narrowest brands of politics.

One religious broadcaster told his audience that if they didn't vote, "You're going to be guilty of murder. You're going to be guilty of an abomination of God. You're going to be guilty for every baby that's aborted from this election forward."[4] This same broadcaster announced that Ted Cruz was "called and anointed to be the next president of the United States."

Pastors laid hands on Donald Trump, wrapped him in prayer shawls, called him "anointed," and compared him to some of the greatest leaders in history. Many clergy echoed former Congressperson Michele Bachmann's contention that God had "raised up" Donald Trump to be president.[5] A rabbi even claimed he had found the Hebrew word for "president" (*nasi*) next to the Hebrew word for "Donald" coded in the book of Deuteronomy.[6]

Clergy on the other side of the aisle were equally outspoken. A Pew Forum survey concluded that 28 percent of those who attended black Protestant churches during one period of the 2016 campaign season heard their pastors speak in support of Hillary Clinton. More than 20 percent heard comments critical of Trump from the pulpit.[7]

So fiercely held were political opinions on every side that some religious leaders were punished for speaking out. Pastor and bestselling

Christian author Max Lucado criticized Donald Trump in a blog and immediately faced a firestorm of criticism and coordinated efforts to boycott his books. Oddly, the comments that enraged millions were relatively mild.

> I don't know Mr. Trump. But I've been chagrined at his antics.
>
> He ridiculed a war hero. He made mockery of a reporter's menstrual cycle. He made fun of a disabled reporter. He referred to the former first lady Barbara Bush as "mommy," and belittled Jeb Bush for bringing her on the campaign trail. He routinely calls people "stupid," "loser," and "dummy." These were not off-line, backstage, overheard, not-to-be-repeated comments. They were publicly and intentionally tweeted, recorded, and presented.[8]

Russell Moore, head of the Southern Baptist Ethics and Religious Liberty Commission, nearly lost his job with his denomination over his comments about Trump. In an article for the *New York Times* entitled, "A White Church No More," Moore called for white Christian Americans to be concerned about racism.

He closed the article with a controversial sentence: "The man on the throne in heaven is a dark-skinned, Aramaic-speaking 'foreigner' who is probably not all that impressed by chants of 'Make America great again.'"[9] Immediately, Trump tweeted that Moore was "a nasty guy with no heart." Baptist leaders around the country joined in. Months after the election, some Baptist megachurches were still announcing their intention to defund the Ethics and Religious Liberty Commission over Moore's comments.[10]

Yet of all the efforts by clergy to spiritually repackage Donald Trump, little had equal impact to the claim that he is a modern version of Cyrus the Great. This was much urged by some religious leaders during the 2016 election and it took root largely because it was an argument for Trump taken from the same Bible millions of religious conservatives held in their hands. To understand this claim and its impact, it is essential to ponder the story of Cyrus the Great from the pages of that same Bible.

His name was Kurus. The ancient Hebrews called him Koresh. The ancient Greeks called him Kyros.

He was a mess. Perhaps this was because his grandfather feared his destiny and tried to have him killed. Perhaps it was because he lived in exile until he was ten years old. That's when he had a playmate who would not obey his commands nearly beaten to death.[11] It caused his secret to get out.

He was Cyrus, son of Cambyses, grandson of Cyrus I. We know him today as Cyrus the Great. He was best known in his own day as "King of the Four Corners of the World."

He is set apart in history not only by the vast empire he ruled but also by the odd decision, so the Bible recounts, of the God of the Jews to use him for noble purposes. He was a vile man, after all. He crushed entire nations under his feet. He tortured his enemies. He worshiped gods of fire and stone. He made the deities of the nations he conquered his own. To the Jews, he was unclean in every way.

Yet, as the Old Testament presents the story, the God of these same Jews said of Cyrus that he had "stirred up one from the east, calling him in righteousness to his service."[12] At least that's what their prophets told them.

It was too horrific to contemplate, the Hebrew people thought. Surely no holy God could use such a detestable man and his bloodthirsty armies.

"He is my shepherd," the God of Israel answered through his prophet Isaiah, "and will accomplish all that I please; he will say of Jerusalem, 'Let it be rebuilt,' and of the temple, 'Let its foundations be laid.'"[13]

It got worse. God intended to clean up the great pagan. "I will raise up Cyrus in my righteousness: I will make all his ways straight.

He will rebuild my city and set my exiles free, but not for a price or a reward, says the LORD Almighty."[14]

Thus did the great Jehovah speak to Israel of Cyrus. Yet he was not done. He wished to speak directly to Cyrus as well.

> This is what the LORD says to his anointed,
>   to Cyrus, whose right hand I will take hold of
> to subdue nations before him
>   and to strip kings of their armor,
> to open doors before him
>   so that gates will not be shut:
> I will go before you
>   and will level mountains;
> I will break down gates of bronze
>   and cut through bars of iron.
> I will give you hidden treasures,
>   riches stored in secret places,
> so that you may know that I am the LORD,
>   the God of Israel, who summons you by name.[15]

So it was that the righteous God of Israel would enlist an idolatrous king into his service. He would make the man clean. He would call him a shepherd. He would anoint him and give him authority to restore the true worship of God. This is how it would be. The Lord God of Israel had spoken.

In the memory of Israel, it all happened as foretold. Cyrus the Great conquered Babylon. He freed the Israelites who had been held there for seventy years. He helped them return to their land, rebuild their temple, and restore their worship. To this day, Cyrus is remembered and celebrated in Jewish liturgy as one chosen of God.

In the 2016 presidential race, millions of Americans came to believe that Donald Trump, just like Cyrus the Great, was a vile, idolatrous man chosen by God. Intriguingly, this idea took root among a people who for eight years had decried Barack Obama as a man with no genuine faith in a genuine God.

Yet the idea appealed because of what it allowed the faithful to believe about Donald Trump. If he was indeed chosen, if he was indeed a modern Cyrus the Great, then it did not matter that he had celebrated his sexual conquests openly on cable TV, that his language was vile, that his treatment of women was sometimes obscene, or that he often spoke in racially offensive terms. God could call him. God could make him righteous. God could anoint him and empower him to restore the true and the pure to the people of God. He had done it with Cyrus many years ago. Perhaps now, in these dire times, God might choose to do it again.

And then Donald Trump won. To millions of Americans, it seemed a miracle. He had defeated a dozen and a half Republican primary opponents with deeper spiritual résumés than his and he bested Hillary Clinton, one of the most religiously outspoken politicians of our time. Surely, Trump was destined. Surely, he would restore the nation as God ordained.

This is a matter of faith. There is no arguing with it. People either believe it or they don't. There is no science and there are no facts that make a difference to this view.

Yet those who hold the Trump as Cyrus the Great Theory, particularly those religious leaders who embrace it, find in it no mandate to call for change. Trump is simply predestined. God will use him as he wills. There is no need to challenge him or insist that he be a better man. No, God was working. Trump had to be vile. The faithful had to accept it and cheer him on. Political victory was confirmation of it all.

It was a view that removed the need for speaking truth to power. Why take the risk? Leave it all to God. There was no need to maintain prophetic distance. There was no need to call a destined man to greater character and compassion.

There were those religious leaders, though, who modeled prophetic distance in the 2016 campaign and who saw much good come of it. One of them was Paul Marc Goulet, pastor of the International Church of Las Vegas.[16]

Goulet was born in Canada and spent his early professional life largely in Asia and Europe. In 1992, he took the lead of a small Las Vegas church and decided to give it an international focus. Two and a half decades later, the church numbered six thousand members, 30 percent of whom are Hispanic and another 30 percent of whom are African-American. Politically, most of the congregation members are either libertarian or independent.

Because he led a large church in Las Vegas and because Republicans hoped to put Nevada in play in 2016, Goulet received calls from nearly every presidential candidate. Would he endorse? Could a given candidate speak at his church? Would he turn his people out in support? They were the usual requests. Candidates and their campaign staffs do their homework. They know their demographics and they know, particularly, what large gatherings occur and where. In most states, megachurches host the largest gatherings other than those at major concerts and sporting events. A pastor like Goulet is besieged.

He decided in the early running to support Ben Carson. He knew him as a man of faith. He liked the way he handled himself. He thought the man had a good chance for a win. He also liked that Carson was African-American. When Carson dropped out and supported Trump, Goulet found himself in crisis. He was troubled by Donald Trump's public manner. Many members of his congregation were also offended with the man for his harsh rhetoric and racist tone. Goulet, who is pro-life, could not support Hillary Clinton. There were no good options at the time, Goulet believed.

Soon after this, a Hispanic leader in Goulet's church was invited to one of the many meetings at Trump Tower designed to introduce the candidate to influencers and to test the waters on specific issues. When the date of the meeting arrived, Goulet's team member, a man named Pasqual Urrabazo, was surprised to find himself sitting next to Trump.

During a question and answer session, Urrabazo, who was the only pastor in the room, had opportunity to tell Trump that he was offended by him. Horrible things had been said about Hispanics. Trump's position on immigration was wrong, Urrabazo said, and it was obvious that the billionaire had no understanding of Hispanic Americans.

What came next surprised Urrabazo. Trump was silent for a while, and then said, "So what do I do? How do I get to know your people?"

Urrabazo did not hesitate. He told Trump that Barack Obama had connected with Hispanics by breaking bread with them. Trump would have to do the same. He would have to humble himself and step into the Hispanic community.

Trump responded immediately. "Good. Then I want to go to your church." Urrabazo was pleased but said he would have to check with Goulet.

Just as Urrabazo returned to Las Vegas, calls from the Trump campaign started reaching Goulet. Could Donald Trump speak at Las Vegas International Church? Goulet said no. This was a shock both to Trump's representatives and to some members of Goulet's church.

His reasoning was that he had already dealt with fallout from working with Ben Carson. Since his congregation was comprised largely of libertarians and independents, any GOP candidate Goulet touted would be an offense to most of his people. He also wasn't sure about Trump. The man was bombastic. He had offended blacks. He had offended Hispanics. He had little civility about him and left scorched earth wherever he went. Why let the man set off bombs during Goulet's Sunday morning services?

No, Donald Trump could not speak at Last Vegas International Church.

The Trump people were persistent. They kept trying to find a way in. They had a mandate from their candidate to put him among

Hispanics like Urrabazo so he could heal the damage he had done. Don't take no for an answer.

Finally, a Trump staffer asked if Goulet's church had a school their candidate could visit. They did. It was exceptional. It even included a sports academy modeled on the European sports club model. It was already famous around the state. Yes, Trump could visit the school. Goulet decided that while he would not allow the candidate to make a mess in his church, he would do what he could to expand Trump's understanding of who evangelicals are and what they hope to embed in the next generation.

And Trump came. When he arrived and got out of his car, he saw Pasqual first. "I told you I'd come!" he said, proud as ever of keeping his word.

The tour began. It had many of the elements common to all tours of schools by politicians. Choirs of students welcomed Trump by singing "God Bless America." The candidate joined hundreds of children half his size in saying the Pledge of Allegiance. Students were urged to shake the candidate's hand.

Yet this was different from anything Trump had experienced before. Yes, he was awarded yet another Bible. Yes, pastors asked if they could pray. All of this had happened before. But Pasqual made sure the candidate met real Las Vegas, not just the white-bread version ever-present in suburban megachurches. A highly decorated Hispanic veteran, prosthetic devices clearly in view, talked to Trump about how he had survived and how Jesus had gotten him through. Trump was interested and held up his entourage and security team to talk to the man at length. He did the same with the groups of black and Hispanic students who gathered around him. They asked him questions, told him they disagreed with him, and hugged him as they turned to go. Trump was visibly moved.

The church had long ministered to Vegas gang members. It was risky and meant some interesting looking people showed up on Sunday mornings. Some of these approached Trump during the tour.

The secret service agents, Trump's private security team, and the local Las Vegas police tensed up and leaned in. The spokesperson was a young man named Troy Martinez. Years before he would have been a threat. Now, he simply wanted to know if Mr. Trump would mind if he and his friends anointed him with oil.

"Sure," Trump said. "I'd love to receive the anointing."

Though by that time he may have had more olive oil rubbed on him in "anointing services" than any other candidate alive, he stood still once again and let converted gangbangers and former barrio hoods pray for God's blessing and power to be upon him.

It was time for the candidate to go. There had been no endorsement. None had been promised. Trump had wanted to connect with Pasqual Urrabazo's Hispanic tribe. Goulet wanted Trump to see a version of evangelicalism he might not have known before. It had been a good day for all.

It was what followed just after that Goulet later remembered most. First, there was the Vegas police officer who approached Goulet and said, "We are afraid of being shot every day. This is the first place we've been where people actually prayed for us." He said he would never be the same.

The amazement of the students, staff, and parents also remained with Goulet. "Trump is nicer in person than he is on stage," people kept whispering to each other. "He's a big man, much taller than he looks on TV, but he's so gentle and kind one-on-one."

It was the media, though, that Goulet would never forget. He had heard Trump complain about them and thought his protests might be overdone. He was stunned, though, by the way journalists handled a candidate's simple visit to a local school. A breathless journalist rushed up to Goulet to ask what he thought about the protests over Trump's visit. Goulet knew there hadn't been any. A Nevada paper even dared the headline, "Trump Terrorizes Second Grade Class." One journalist intimated that Trump had paid Goulet off for allowing the visit. Only the Reuters news agency conducted itself respectably,

Goulet realized. The behavior of the rest made him wonder if he had ever heard the truth about Donald Trump.

A few months later, Pastor Goulet was speaking at a Saturday event in Dallas when he received a call from his wife, Denise.

"Trump wants to come to church tomorrow," she said.

"No," Goulet responded. "It will disrupt everything! This is exactly what I wanted to avoid."

"He's going to come secretly," she told him. "We don't have to do the whole security thing. He'll come incognito. He even offered to sit in back. He just wants to come to church."

This gave Goulet pause. He thought back over Trump's earlier visit. He realized the man must have been touched. Why else would he ask to visit the church again without caring if he was seen?

Then Goulet had an idea. The video of Trump speaking in raunchy terms about women was all over the news. Goulet knew it was vile and had said publicly that this kind of treatment of women was contrary to everything he believed. Yet if Trump wanted to visit again, he was going to see a different set of values on full display.

"Okay. Let him come," Goulet said to Denise. "But you preach. I want him to see God use a woman like he so often uses you." This was no challenge. Denise Goulet was the church's senior associate pastor and was a gifted speaker. "I want Trump to never forget what righteous womanhood is. You preach. Honor him. Pray over him. It's your time to shine."

That next day, Donald Trump did visit Las Vegas International Church. At Denise's insistence, he sat on the front row next to her. Trump participated in worship and listened to "Pastor Denise" teach the Bible. At one point, he was asked to join her on the stage.

"May we have the honor of praying for you?" Denise asked.

"Yes. Of course." And while the church prayed, Trump became visibly emotional.

He had been fascinated by the service from the moment he walked in. Moved during worship, he turned to Denise and said, "I'm going to fight the Johnson Amendment. The church has to have its voice back." It was as though this was the best gift Trump could give.

Denise thanked him.

A few moments later, Trump asked, "Do you love what you do?"

Denise said she did, but the question caused her to utter a prayer: "God, who is this man?"

Finally, Trump turned to her and said, "Listen, you're doing an amazing job."

This second experience with Donald Trump was everything Goulet hoped it would be. He would not endorse Trump. He would not ask for money, though later Trump sent an unsolicited donation. He would also never accept a position in the campaign even if it were offered. He would, though, welcome the man into his family of faith. He would allow him to hear the gospel of Christ taught by a woman. He would allow him to know the intercessions of former convicts, of ex–Vegas gang members, of women who were once strippers and were now raising Christian families, and of a people of far different political views.

He would not endorse Donald Trump, but he was happy to show him a facet of faith he perhaps had not seen before. In doing so, Goulet had done what a fellow religious leader had once described: "I won't endorse candidates. But I will give them a chance to hear truth and see it in action. I will show them a picture of what, with God's help, they might be."

This is the art of prophetic distance.

Epilogue

On the first night of the Republican National Convention in July 2016, Melania Trump gave the keynote address. It was the first such speech she had ever given and much of the nation was eager to hear from the quiet, pretty woman so often at Donald Trump's side. Given her glamorous manner and the historic import of the evening, the speech ought to have been a glowing success.

It wasn't.

Though the speech was widely praised in the first hours after it was given, it soon gave up its secrets. There was language in it taken almost word for word from Michelle Obama's 2008 convention speech. Particularly embarrassing was that the words borrowed pertained to how Melania felt about her parents and her children, about hopes for the future and matters of right and wrong. These were personal reflections. Why, the nation's media wondered aloud, couldn't she be authentic about expressing such individual feelings? Why borrow from the one person on the planet from whom she most needed to distinguish herself?

It was a loss, and not just politically. Given Melania Trump's story, any speechwriter worth the name could have produced a moving talk. She was born in communist Yugoslavia in 1970. She lived under tyrannical rule and as a child watched the swirl of world events impact life within view of her family's front door. Her talents distinguished her, she became an immigrant in a world new to her, and she ended up marrying a rich and powerful man who would one day be his nation's president.

She was also sensitive. She had abandoned social media because she abhorred its "negativity." She felt deeply for children growing up in a bullying, mocking world. As First Lady, she hoped to exhibit the style of a Jackie Kennedy and to serve the greater good like Betty Ford. She was also an engaging realist. Asked about her husband's constant Twitter wars, she told reporters that she had tried to get him to stop but that in the end, the man would "do what he wants to do."

She was worthy of a great speech. It ought to have been hers. The nation—even her political enemies—ought to have had opportunity to exult in a moving story and to enjoy half an hour with a beautiful woman and her heartfelt, accented thoughts about the world.

The culture of the Trump campaign prevented it. This was largely due, of course, to Donald Trump. He had no patience with experts and professor-types whom he thought were always in his way. Bureaucrats seemed always in his way. Consultants, specialists, and those academically trained rarely knew as much he thought he did about his business and the way things ought to work. He learned to work around them.

This is what happened with Melania's speech. Family members pitched in. Campaign officials offered some ideas. A few drafts were written months before that night. No one was put in charge. The team of speechwriters who usually serve a potential First Lady was never engaged. The campaign explained that Melania wanted to write the speech on her own. So staffers assembled some raw material, including the better sections of Michelle Obama's highly regarded speech. The plagiarism was largely inadvertent. It didn't matter. The embarrassment drowned out the good an otherwise fine talk might have done.

It was all because of Team Trump's underlying suspicions. It was all because no one of experience was trusted with final authority. Keep the experts at bay. We do better on our own. We can do at least as well as the smart guys and with a whole lot less hassle along the way.

It was a failure born of combativeness. It was a misfire caused by too much concern for competition. It was undergirded by anger and wrapped in supreme self-confidence. And the poetry was lost. A woman's tender story and its tribute to the nation were lost. All because of a culture around Donald Trump that is ever at war with the world.

Yet this is exactly what those who voted for him loved about Donald Trump. He was as angry as they were. He was as fed up with talking heads and indecisive politicians and traitorous corporations as they could ever be. He might not be the kind of man they would want their daughters to date, but he would give them back their nation. Besides, their preachers said Mr. Trump might be chosen by God. He might be a Cyrus or a Lincoln or a Churchill. No need to worry about his distortions or his morals or what he thought of people of color.

It was the anger that mattered. His supporters felt they were losing their place in a nation slipping away. The numbers help to tell this tale. The average age of a Trump voter was fifty-seven years of age. Nine in ten of them were white. Most had no college degree.

This was different from the broader nation. The average American is thirty-eight years old. They are attending college at a rapidly rising rate. More than a third of them are non-white.[1]

There is a rift, then, on the demographic landscape of American society. Change is coming. A younger tribe is stepping to the fore. An older one is not always happy about it. And this older tribe still has time to play a role. In an age when people routinely live into their nineties, decades remain to those in their fifties. The American rift is not soon going away.

To the extent that the Trump presidency is built upon eternal principles and timeworn truth, it may accomplish noble things and engage large portions of the nation. To the extent it is small, angry, vindictive, and grasping, it may fulfill H. L. Mencken's prophecy of nearly a century ago. "As democracy is perfected," the eminent journalist wrote, "the office of the president represents, more and more closely, the inner soul of the people. On some great and glorious day, the plain folk of the land will reach their heart's desire at last, and the White House will be occupied by a downright fool and a complete narcissistic moron."[2]

We hope for better. And it may occur. There are some good people around Donald Trump, patriots of competence and serious purpose. They may prevail. Presidential administrations are defined by the tension between the better angels of human nature and the lesser spirits that lurk in the dark. The dark side has often had an upper hand in the world of Donald Trump. Perhaps there is opportunity for a change.

Some, but not all, of this is in the hands of the religious voices Trump allows a hearing. If they are courageous, if they are true, they may help to guide the ship of state to safe and prosperous harbors. If they do not, they may pay a great price and draw the ire of later generations for being cowardly and unprincipled—all while owning Donald Trump.

Acknowledgments

This book was written during a tumultuous time in American history. Donald Trump had just been elected president of the United States. His inauguration was widely celebrated and just as widely condemned in massive, angry demonstrations. His first acts in office were cheered as essential steps in making America great again and grieved as acts of intentional destruction to American democracy.

In the interviews I conducted for writing this book, I spoke with patriots who wept at the thought of a Trump presidency and with patriots who could not contain their glee. I listened to Christians who broke into prayer against Donald Trump in the middle of our time together and to Christians who marveled that any of their fellow believers did not share their pro-Trump views. I also spoke with the terrified: aging Hispanics, young black students, and beloved Muslim Kurdish friends, as well as friends who are gay, handicapped, immigrants, and serving on the frontlines of America's armed conflicts around the world.

In other words, I spoke to a cross-section of America. I'm grateful to all who shared their stories, their hopes, and their time with me.

There were numerous members of the Trump transition team and new administration who discussed the themes in this book with me but who asked not to be identified. I understood. They were living through a presidential handoff in which every syllable they uttered became part of the intensifying fray. I was moved by their hopes for the new administration and stirred by their sacrifices. Their imprint upon these pages is profound.

I was saddened by those who refused to speak with me, particularly those who have been happy to help me with previous books. Some of these friends have been so beat up for taking a stand during the 2016 campaign that they simply could not bring themselves to face the barrage again. Some were unsure of their former positions and wanted time to rethink. A few were simply cowardly, and all the more so given their loud pronouncements during one of the most transitional elections in American history. All of these, though, are loved and welcomed in my life.

Barely two weeks after the 2016 election, I listened to Reverend Al Sharpton explain the difference between the presidency defined by Barack Obama's *Dreams from My Father* and the presidency soon to be defined by Donald Trump's *The Art of the Deal*. Rev. Sharpton was both fierce and kind and I am grateful for the time he spent helping this white man understand.

I will never forget my conversation with Jim Wallis of *Sojourners*. His rich voice drenched with grief, he was the Old Testament prophet bemoaning the racism of the Trump campaign. It was as though he was a wizened Aslan setting himself against abuse of the hurting and downtrodden. This is not the first time he has helped me to see the world through his eyes. I am a better man for every moment spent under his tutelage.

Dr. Robert Jeffress of First Baptist Church in Dallas took time to explain his early endorsement of Donald Trump and his belief that a secular billionaire may yet become the most faith-friendly president in American history. He spoke to me just days before he gave the Inauguration Day sermon at St. John's Church in Washington, DC. His time was precious then and I am grateful he chose to spend some of it with me.

Ed Stetzer, executive director of the Billy Graham Center for Evangelism, has long been a friend, and I never cease to be amazed at his knowledge of the religious underpinnings of American culture. He was wise, insightful, and ever the iconoclast in our time together, and I am grateful he is in the world and in my life.

Paul Marc Goulet, pastor of International Church of Las Vegas, spent time talking to me when he was supposed to be walking a California beach recovering from a near-death experience. I am sworn to keep this from his doctors and his wife. He brought to our conversation the perspective of one born in Canada, experienced in Europe, certified in counseling and therapy, and seasoned by years of growing a large and socially relevant church in Las Vegas. I am grateful for his time and also that there are people like him filling America's pulpits.

Dr. George Grant has been both mentor and older brother/friend to me for many years. His scholarship, deeply Reformed faith, humor, and gentleness have shaped my life, and I cannot express my gratitude fully in this life. He spoke with me at length about his distinctly Christian version of the Never Trump movement and I was both instructed and challenged, as I always am, by his thinking. He is a modern Thomas Chalmers and it is a privilege for me even to be in his presence.

Johnnie Moore, CEO of the Kairos Company, helped me immensely with this book. He has been an eyewitness to much of the early history of the Trump administration. His insights, his storyteller's gifts, and his wise judgment have proven invaluable.

Honor is due to Baker Books for trusting their author. This is a dangerous book. It critiques a sitting president, dares to prod internationally influential religious leaders, and takes seriously a man despised by more than half the population of the United States and most of the world. Still, they have courageously stayed in harness and brought their skills to bear on what is sure to be a controversial book. I am grateful they have chosen to live out the best of the Reformed tradition in calling civil magistrates to their godly best. Thanks in particular are due to Chad Allen, who felt the heat on more than one occasion.

I am grateful, as ever, to Chartwell Literary Group and the merry band of editors and consultants they summoned to action on behalf of this book, Isaac Darnall in particular. I cannot imagine crafting literature without the aid of this unique firm. Deepest thanks to them for what they have meant to my career.

My executive assistant, Karen Montgomery, makes my business world work. She is far too qualified to work with me, but I am trusting that no one will dare tell her and so lift her deception. She not only expertly edited this book and gave vital input but also ran our growing firm with skill. I am grateful for her gifts and I apologize to her husband, David, for stealing her from him so often.

Strategic support of a different kind was provided by dear friends Jim Laffoon and Jim Critcher. Many writers run on the fuel of ego. Some are energized purely by their subjects and the writing experience itself. I run largely on the belief that I can do some good in the world by what I write. Messrs. Laffoon and Critcher point me toward this goal. They remind me of who I am, remind me of the needs of our generation, and remind me of what an idiot I can sometimes be. I am grateful for their friendship but, even more, I am grateful for their older brother insights into my soul and the gentle way they guide me past the shoals.

When my children were young, they regarded each book I wrote as a thief. All they knew was that something on Dad's desk robbed time from our wrestling and making cookies and learning new ways to tickle. Fortunately, they forgave these crimes. Now they join me in the work of putting words on the page. They have grown into gracious souls and fine minds and it is a father's joy to have them at my side. Both Jonathan and Elizabeth read this book and gave suggestions. They grant me a new generation's wisdom. Love and gratitude to both of you guys.

Finally, deepest affection to my wife, Beverly, who has restored me and who graces all things in my life with her love and her beauty. *Amor Vincit Omnia.*

Donald Trump in His Own Words

Those waiting for Donald Trump to be a skilled speechmaker will be waiting a long time. He is not likely ever to acquire the grace of Kennedy, the delivery of Reagan, or the depth of Lincoln. He is too much the New York tough guy and has been too long in the presence of men like Roy Cohn to manage even smoothness in his speech, much less poetry.

He is also his own worst enemy. He resists working from notes. He interrupts himself constantly. He likes playful interaction with the crowd that can be endearing but also breaks up his cadence and the flow of his thought. We can expect the mental breakdown of several speechwriters should Trump hold office for more than four years!

He is not unlike a grizzled New York construction crew foreman trying to tell his workers that his daughter is getting married. He's emotional. He covers this with joking and jabs at a few of his men. He loves his daughter but knows the construction site is no place for tears or fluffy talk. Trump is the same. He loves his country and his cause, but he must always be the gruff boss to hold his own. His message comes in between the jabs and the bluster, like the calm between bursts of machine-gun fire.

Still, there can be depth and beauty in his speeches and not just from the craft of his speechwriters. Two Trump talks are good examples. When he spoke at the National Prayer Breakfast just weeks after being inaugurated, he joked about praying for Arnold Schwarzenegger and the declining fortunes of the reality TV show *The Apprentice*. He also swore at one point. It was nearly all the media chose to remember. Yet there are side comments and core text that reveal much of what Trump thinks about religion and the nation. It is worth recalling and, given Trump's style of delivery, is better digested from a transcript than live.

The same is true of the talk Trump gave to a largely African-American church in Detroit in September 2016. He was the Republican nominee then. The event was much criticized because it was hosted by an African-American bishop known for preaching a prosperity-oriented gospel and because Trump was given a Jewish prayer shawl, a *tallit*, as a gift. None of this played well with media, with some Jews, or with many mainstream Christians afterward.

What was missed in the firestorm of controversy was that Trump had written his remarks himself. They were heartfelt, gently delivered, and evidence of the Republican nominee trying to reach across the divide to Black America. His words are punctuated with the occasional "So true" or "So important," his way of adding emphasis and attempting connection. As with the words of his National Prayer Breakfast talk, the meaning is best absorbed from the written version. Yet here is genuine Donald Trump, raw but openhearted, ever contentious but with an eye toward the will of God as he perceives it.

Donald Trump at the National Prayer Breakfast[1]

Washington, DC
February 2, 2017

Thank you very much, it's a great honor to be here this morning. And so many faith leaders—very, very important people to me—from across our magnificent nation, and so many leaders from all across the globe. Today we continue a tradition begun by President Eisenhower some 64 years ago. This gathering is a testament to the power of faith and is one of the great customs of our nation. And I hope to be here seven more times with you.

(APPLAUSE)

I want very much to thank our co-chair Senator Boozman and Senator Coons. And all of the congressional leadership; they're all over the place. We have a lot of very distinguished guests. And we have one guest who was just sworn in last night, Rex Tillerson, secretary of state.

(APPLAUSE)

Gonna do a great job.

(APPLAUSE)

Some people didn't like Rex because he actually got along with leaders of the world. I said, no, you have to understand that's a good thing. That's a good thing, not a bad thing. He's respected all over the world and I think he's going to go down as one of our great, great secretaries.

We appreciate it.

Thank you, thank you, Rex.

(APPLAUSE)

Thank you as well to Senate Chaplain Barry Black, for his moving words. And I don't know Chaplain whether or not that's an appointed position—is that an appointed position? I don't even know if you're Democrat or if you're Republican, but I'm appointing you for another year, the hell with it.

(LAUGHTER)

And I think it's not even my appointment, it's the Senate's appointment, but we'll talk to them. You're very—you're—your son is here. Your job is very, very secure. OK?

(LAUGHTER)

Thank you, Barry. Appreciate it very much.

I also want to thank my great friends the Roma. Where's Roma? Beautiful Roma Downey, the voice of an angel. She's got the voice—every time I hear that voice; it's so beautiful. That—everything is so beautiful about Roma, including her husband because he's a special, special friend. Mark Burnett for the wonderful introduction.

So true, so true. I said to the agent, I'm sorry, the only thing wrong—I actually got on the phone and fired him myself because he said, you don't want to do it, it'll never work, it'll never, ever work, you don't want to do it. I said, listen. When I really fired him after it became the number one show, it became so successful and he wanted a commission and he didn't want to this.

That's when I really said—but we had tremendous success on *The Apprentice*. And when I ran for president, I had to leave the show. That's when I knew for sure that I was doing it. And they hired a big, big movie star, Arnold Schwarzenegger, to take my place. And we know how that turned out. The ratings went down the tubes. It's been a total disaster and Mark will never, ever bet against Trump again. And I want to just pray for Arnold if we can, for those ratings, OK?

(LAUGHTER)

But we've had an amazing life together the last 14, 15 years. And a—an outstanding man and thank you very much for introducing. Appreciate it. It's a great honor.

I also want to thank my dear friend, Vice President Mike Pence, who has been incredible.

(APPLAUSE)

And incredible wife, Karen.

And every time I was in a little trouble with something where they were questioning me, they'd say, "But he picked Mike Pence."

(LAUGHTER)

"So he has to know what he's doing."

(LAUGHTER)

And it's true, he's been—you know on the scale of zero to 10, I rate him a 12, OK?

So I want to thank you, thank you very much, appreciate it.

(APPLAUSE)

But most importantly, today I wanna thank the American people. Your faith and prayers have sustained me and inspired me through some very, very tough times. All around America, I have met amazing people whose words of worship and encouragement have been a constant source of strength.

What I hear most often as I travel the country are five words that never, ever fail to touch my heart, that's "I am praying for you." I hear it so often, I am praying for you, Mr. President.

(APPLAUSE)

No one has inspired me more in my travels than the families of the United States military. Men and women who have put their lives on the line every day for their country and their countrymen. I just came back yesterday, from Dover Air Force Base, to join the family of Chief William "Ryan" Owens as America's fallen hero was returned home.

Very, very sad, but very, very beautiful, very, very beautiful. His family was there, incredible family, loved him so much, so devastated, he was so devastated, but the ceremony was amazing. He died in defense of our nation. He gave his life in defense of our people. Our debt to him and our debt to his family is eternal and everlasting. "Greater love hath no man than this, that a man lay down his life for his friends."

We will never forget the men and women who wear the uniform, believe me.

(APPLAUSE)

Thank you.

(APPLAUSE)

From generation to generation, their vigilance has kept our liberty alive. Our freedom is won by their sacrifice and our security has been earned with their sweat and blood and tears. God has blessed this land to give us such incredible heroes and patriots. They are very, very special and we are going to take care of them.

(APPLAUSE)

Our soldiers understand that what matters is not party or ideology or creed, but the bonds of loyalty that link us all together as one. America is a nation of believers. In towns all across our land, it's plain to see what we easily forget—so easily we forget this, that the quality of our lives is not defined by our material success, but by our spiritual success.

I will tell you that and I tell you that from somebody that has had material success and known tremendous numbers of people with great material success, the most material success. Many of those people are very, very miserable, unhappy people.

And I know a lot of people without that, but they have great families. They have great faith; they don't have money, at least, not nearly to the extent. And they're happy. Those, to me, are the successful people, I have to tell you.

(APPLAUSE)

I was blessed to be raised in a churched home. My mother and father taught me that to whom much is given, much is expected. I was sworn in on the very Bible from which my mother would teach us as young children, and that faith lives on in my heart every single day.

The people in this room come from many, many backgrounds. You represent so many religions and so many views. But we are all united by our faith, in our creator and our firm knowledge that we are all equal in His eyes. We are not just flesh and bone and blood, we are human beings with souls. Our republic was formed on the basis that freedom is not a gift from government, but that freedom is a gift from God.

(APPLAUSE)

It was the great Thomas Jefferson who said, the God who gave us life, gave us liberty. Jefferson asked, can the liberties of a nation be secure when we have removed a conviction that these liberties are the gift of God[?] Among those freedoms is the right to worship according to our own beliefs. That is why I will get rid of and totally destroy the Johnson Amendment and allow our representatives of faith to speak freely and without fear of retribution. I will do that, remember.

(APPLAUSE)

Freedom of religion is a sacred right, but it is also a right under threat all around us, and the world is under serious, serious threat in so many different ways. And I've never seen it so much and so openly as since I took the position of president.

The world is in trouble, but we're going to straighten it out. OK? That's what I do. I fix things. We're going to straighten it out.

(APPLAUSE)

Believe me. When you hear about the tough phone calls I'm having, don't worry about it. Just don't worry about it. They're tough. We have to [be] tough. It's time we're going to be a little tough folks. We're taking [sic] advantage of by every nation in the world virtually. It's not going to happen anymore. It's not going to happen anymore. We have seen unimaginable violence carried out in the name of religion. Acts of wantonness (ph) (inaudible) just minorities. Horrors on a scale that defy description. Terrorism is a fundamental threat to religious freedom. It must be stopped and it will be stopped. It may not be pretty for a little while. It will be stopped. We have seen . . .

(APPLAUSE)

And by the way, General, as you know James "Mad Dog," shouldn't say it in this room, Mattis, now there's a reason they call him "Mad Dog" Mattis, never lost a battle, always wins them, and always wins them fast. He's our new secretary of defense, will be working with Rex. He's right now in South Korea, going to Japan, going to some other spots. I'll tell you what, I've gotten to know him really well. He's the real deal. We have somebody who's the real deal working for us and that's what we need. So, you watch. You just watch.

(APPLAUSE)

Things will be different. We have seen peace loving Muslims brutalize[d], victimize[d], murdered, and oppressed by ISIS killers. We have seen threats of extermination against the Jewish people. We have seen a campaign of ISIS and genocide against Christians, where they cut off heads. Not since the Middle Ages have we seen that. We haven't seen that, the cutting off of heads. Now they cut off the heads, they drown people in steel cages. Haven't seen this. I haven't seen this. Nobody's seen this for many, many years.

All nations have a moral obligation to speak out against such violence. All nations have a duty to work together to confront it and to confront it viciously if we have to.

So I want to express clearly today, to the American people, that my administration will do everything in its power to defend and protect religious liberty in our land. America must forever remain a tolerant society where all face [sic] are respected and where all of our citizens can feel safe and secure. We have to feel safe and secure. In recent days, we have begun to take necessary action to achieve that goal. Our nation has the most generous immigration system in the world. But these are those and there are those that would exploit that generosity to undermine the values that we hold so dear. We need security.

There are those who would seek to enter our country for the purpose of spreading violence, or oppressing other people based upon their faith or their lifestyle, not right. We will not allow a beachhead of intolerance to spread in our nation. You look all over the world and you see what's happening. So in the coming days, we will develop a system to help ensure that those admitted into our country fully embrace our values of religious and personal liberty. And that they reject any form of oppression and discrimination. We want people to come into our nation, but we want people to love us and to love our values, not to hate us and to hate our values.

We will be a safe country, we will be a free country and we will be a country where all citizens can practice their beliefs without fear of hostility or a fear of violence. America will flourish, as long as our liberty, and in particular, our religious liberty is allowed to flourish.

(APPLAUSE.)

America will succeed, as long as our most vulnerable citizens— and we have some that are so vulnerable—have a path to success. And America will thrive, as long as we continue to have faith in each other and faith in God.

(APPLAUSE)

That faith in God has inspired men and women to sacrifice for the needy, to deploy to wars overseas and to lock arms at home, to ensure equal rights for every man, woman and child in our land. It's that faith that sent the pilgrims across the oceans, the pioneers across the plains and the young people all across America, to chase their dreams. They are chasing their dreams. We are going to bring those dreams back.

As long as we have God, we are never, ever alone. Whether it's the soldier on the night watch, or the single parent on the night shift, God will always give us solace and strength, and comfort. We need to carry on and to keep carrying on. For us here in Washington, we must never, ever stop asking God for the wisdom to serve the public, according to his will. That's why . . .

(APPLAUSE)

Thank you.

(APPLAUSE)

That's why President Eisenhower and Senator Carlson had the wisdom to gather together 64 years ago, to begin this truly great tradition. But that's not all they did together. Lemme tell you the rest of the story.

Just one year later, Senator Carlson was among the members of Congress to send to the president's desk a joint resolution that added, "Under God," to our Pledge of Allegiance. It's a great thing.

(APPLAUSE)

Because that's what we are and that is what we will always be and that is what our people want; one beautiful nation, under God.

Thank you, God bless you and God bless America. Thank you very much. Thank you.

(APPLAUSE)

Thank you.

(APPLAUSE)

Donald Trump at Great Faith Ministries Church[2]

Detroit, Michigan
September 3, 2016

Thank you. Thank you very much.

(APPLAUSE)

Thank you. That's so nice, thank you.

(APPLAUSE)

Thank you very much.

Well, that's so nice.

And, Bishop Jackson, I want to thank you and Dr. Jackson. And you have some voice, I have to say. Incredible, and some spirit, some spirit. Moved. Talent.

(APPLAUSE)

Thank you.

Well, I just wrote this the other day knowing I'd be here, and I mean it from the heart. And I'd like to just read it. And I think you'll understand it maybe better than I do in certain ways.

For centuries, the African-American church has been the conscience of our country, so true. It's from the pews and pulpits and Christian teachings of black churches all across this land that the civil rights movement lifted up its soul and lifted up the soul of our nation.

It's from these pews that our nation has been inspired toward a better moral character, a deeper concern for mankind, and spirit of charity and unity that binds us all together, and we are bound together, and I see that today. This has been an amazing day for me.

The African-American faith community has been one of God's greatest gifts to America and to its people. There is perhaps no action our leaders can take that would do more to heal our country and support our people than to provide a greater platform to the black churches and churchgoers.

You do right every day by your community and your families. You raise children in the light of God. I will always support your church, always, and defend your right to worship. It's so important.

I am here today to listen to your message, and I hope my presence here will also help your voice to reach new audiences in our country. And many of these audiences desperately need your spirit and your thought, I can tell you that.

Christian faith is not the past, but the present and the future. Make it stronger, we'll make it stronger.

(APPLAUSE)

And we'll open it up to great, great leaders like Pastor Jackson, Bishop Jackson, Dr. Jackson and so many others. And so many others actually sitting here, Darryl Scott, who's phenomenal, who has been with me for so long, so long.

(APPLAUSE)

Omarosa, who's actually a very nice person, but I don't want to say that because I will destroy her image by saying that. But she's actually a very, very fine person and a pastor.

And I just want to thank all of the folks. And there is somebody who's been very special to me, Dr. Ben Carson, who's been—stand up, Ben. Come here.

(APPLAUSE)

Come here, Ben.

This is a great man and a great guy.

(APPLAUSE)

So as I prepare to campaign all across the nation and in every community, I will have an opportunity to lay out my plans for economic change, which will be so good for Detroit and so good for this community because we're going to bring jobs back.

(APPLAUSE)

I will have a chance—thank you. We'll bring them back. We're taking them back from Mexico and everywhere else because they're gone.

I will have a chance to discuss school choice, which is very important, and how to put every American on the ladder to success, a great education and a great job.

But today I just want to let you know that I am here to listen to you. And I've been doing that. And we had a fantastic interview with Bishop Jackson. It was really an amazing interview. He's better than the people who do that professionally, I will tell you, it's true, it's true.

(LAUGHTER)

(APPLAUSE)

It's true. He was better. And I didn't really know what I was getting myself into. I didn't know. Was this going to be nice? Was this going to be wild? He is a great gentleman and a very smart guy. I just hope you don't lose him to Hollywood. That's the only problem. And especially Dr. Jackson, she may be gone. Hollywood is calling, look at all those television cameras back there.

(APPLAUSE)

No, look at all the television cameras. I'm sorry to do that to you, Bishop, because, you know, one of those things, right?

(LAUGHTER)

Our nation is too divided. We talk past each other, not to each other. And those who seek office do not do enough to step into the community and learn what is going on. They don't know, they have no clue.

I'm here today to learn so that we can together remedy injustice in any form and so that we can also remedy economics so that the African-American community can benefit economically through jobs and income and so many other different ways.

Our political system has failed the people and works only to enrich itself. I want to reform that system so that it works for you, everybody in this room. I believe true reform can only come from outside the system. I really mean that. Being a businessman is much different than being a politician because I understand what's happening. And we are going outside the establishment.

Becoming the nominee of the party of Abraham Lincoln—a lot of people don't realize that Abraham Lincoln, the great Abraham Lincoln, was a Republican—has been the greatest honor of my life. It is on his legacy that I hope to build the future of the party, but more important, the future of the country and the community.

I believe we need a civil rights agenda for our time, one that ensures the rights to a great education, so important, and the right to live in safety and in peace and to have a really, really great job, a good-paying job and one that you love to go to every morning. And that can happen. We need to bring our companies back.

It also means the right to have a government that protects our workers and fights, really fights, for our jobs. I want to help you build and rebuild Detroit. And we can do that, especially with people like Bishop Jackson and Dr. Jackson. I mean that.

(APPLAUSE)

It's been an amazing experience. It's been an amazing experience. True.

Nothing is more sad than when we sideline young black men with unfulfilled potential, tremendous potential. I met some people this morning that were incredible people and they're looking for jobs. These are incredible people, young people. Our whole country loses out when we're unable to harness the brilliance and the energy of these folks.

We're one nation. And when anyone hurts, we all hurt together. And that's so true, so true.

(APPLAUSE)

We're all brothers and sisters and we're all created by the same God. We must love each other and support each other, and we are in this all together, all together.

I fully understand that the African-American community has suffered from discrimination and that there are many wrongs that must still be made right. And they will be made right. I want to make America prosperous for everyone. I want to make this city the economic envy of the world, and we can do that, we can do that again.

(APPLAUSE)

Factories everywhere, new roads and bridges, new schools, especially schools, and new hope. I have been so greatly blessed and in so many ways, with no greater blessing than my family. I have a great family. Nothing would make me happier and more fulfilled than to use what I have learned in business and in traveling all over the world, I've sort of seen a lot, to bring the wealth and prosperity and opportunity to those who have not had these opportunities before, and that's many, many people in Detroit.

When I see wages falling, people out of work, I know the hardships this inflicts. And I am determined to do something about it. I will do something about it. I do get things done, I will tell you. Some people have strengths, that's one of mine. I get things done. I'm going to get things done for you.

Please know this. For any who are hurting, things are going to turn around. Tomorrow will be better, it will be much better, what the pastor and I were talking about riding up the street and we see all those closed stores and people sitting down on the sidewalk and no jobs and no activity. We'll get it turned around.

We'll get it turned around, Pastor. Believe me.

(APPLAUSE)

We're going to win again as a country and we're going to win again for all of our people. I want to work with you to renew the bonds of trust between citizens and the bonds of faith that make our nation strong. America's been lifted out of many of its most difficult hours through the miracle of faith and through people like Bishop Jackson and Dr. Jackson. It's so important.

(APPLAUSE)

People have no idea how important they are. Now in these hard times for our country, let us turn again to our Christian heritage to lift up the soul of our nation.

I am so deeply grateful to be here today. And it is my prayer that America of tomorrow, and I mean that, that the America of tomorrow will be one of unity, togetherness and peace. And perhaps we can add the word "prosperity," OK? Prosperity.

(APPLAUSE)

I'd like to conclude with a passage from 1 John 4.

(APPLAUSE)

You know it? See, most groups I speak to don't know that, but we know it.

(LAUGHTER)

If you want, we can say it together. No one has ever seen God, but if we love one another, God lives in us and his love is made complete in us. And that's so true.

(APPLAUSE)

Thank you very much. This has been such an honor. Thank you very much.

Bishop, thank you, sir. Thank you. Thank you.

(APPLAUSE)

Thank you, Bishop.

Thank you.

I like that.

Thank you so much.

Thank you.

Notes

Front Matter

1. Martin Luther King Jr., "A Knock at Midnight," *A Knock at Midnight: Inspiration from the Great Sermons of Reverend Martin Luther King, Jr.* (New York: Grand Central Publishing, 2000), 72–73.

Introduction

1. Colin Campbell, "Donald Trump: 'I Am the Only One Who Can Make American Truly Great Again!'" *Business Insider*, March 18, 2015, http://www .businessinsider.com/donald-trump-i-am-the-only-one-who-can-make-america -truly-great-again-2015-3?op=1.
2. *Everson v. Board of Education of Ewing Tp.*, 330 US at 15 (1947).

Chapter 1 Convergence

1. Donald J. Trump, *Great Again: How to Fix Our Crippled America* (New York: Simon & Schuster, 2015), Kindle loc. 1537–39.
2. Unnamed university official, interview with author, January 17, 2017, Washington, DC.
3. Trump, *Great Again*, Kindle loc. 1535–36.
4. Matthew Schmitz, "Donald Trump, Man of Faith," *First Things*, August 2016.
5. James Barron, "Overlooked Influences on Donald Trump: A Famous Minister and His Church," *New York Times*, September 5, 2016.
6. David Cay Johnston, *The Making of Donald Trump* (Brooklyn: Melville House, 2016), Kindle loc. 296–97.
7. Michael D'Antonio, *The Truth About Trump* (New York: St. Martin's Press, 2016), Kindle loc. 1194–97.
8. Katie Glueck, "Trump's Religious Dealmaking Pays Dividends," *Politico*, December 7, 2016, http://www.politico.com/story/2016/12/trump-religious-deal making-dividends-232277.

9. "Full Speech: Donald Trump Speaks at Liberty University Convocation (1-18-16)," YouTube video, 4:20, posted by Right Side Broadcasting, January 18, 2016, https://www.youtube.com/watch?v=E32ZPa4LGkM.

Chapter 2 Mixture

1. Jesse Byrnes, "Trump: Kerry Probably Hasn't Read the Bible," *The Hill*, February 24, 2016, http://thehill.com/blogs/blog-briefing-room/news/270610-trump-kerry-probably-hasnt-read-the-bible.

2. Jeremy Diamond, "Donald Trump Jumps In: The Donald's Latest White House Run Is Officially On," *CNN Politics*, June 17, 2015, http://www.cnn.com/2015/06/16/politics/donald-trump-2016-announcement-elections/.

3. Johnston, *Making of Donald Trump*, Kindle loc. 394–98.

4. Globe staff, "The Religion of Donald Trump," *Boston Globe*, September 14, 2015, https://www.bostonglobe.com/news/nation/2015/09/14/trumpsidebar/kLTBdwJosIkO4FXfZCzPyL/story.html.

5. Ibid.

6. Ibid.

7. Daniel Burke, "The Guilt-Free Gospel of Donald Trump," CNN.com, October 24, 2016, http://www.cnn.com/2016/10/21/politics/trump-religion-gospel/.

8. Ibid.

9. Jeremy Diamond, "Pastor Interrupts Trump to Stop Him from Attacking Clinton in Church," *CNN Politics*, September 15, 2016, http://www.cnn.com/2016/09/14/politics/donald-trump-pastor-flint-michigan/.

10. McCay Coppins, "The Gospel According to Trump," *New York Times*, January 18, 2016, https://www.nytimes.com/2016/01/18/opinion/campaign-stops/the-gospel-according-to-trump.html.

11. Daniel Burke, "Pope Suggests Trump Is Not a Christian," *CNN Politics*, February 18, 2016, http://www.cnn.com/2016/02/18/politics/pope-francis-trump-christian-wall/index.html.

12. Burke, "The Guilt-Free Gospel of Donald Trump."

13. "There's no way I would ever throw anything, to do anything negative to a Bible, so what we do is we keep all of the Bibles. I would have a fear of doing something other than very positive so actually I store them and keep them and sometimes give them away to other people," as quoted in "Donald Trump: Christianity is a 'Wonderful Religion,'" *Christian Today*, April 12, 2011, https://www.christiantoday.com/article/donald.trump.christianity.is.a.wonderful.religion/27821.htm.

Chapter 3 King

1. Donald J. Trump and Tony Schwartz, *The Art of the Deal* (New York: Ballantine Books, 1987), 71.

2. D'Antonio, *Truth About Trump*, Kindle loc. 931–32.

3. Gwenda Blair, *The Trumps: Three Generations of Builders and a President* (New York: Simon & Schuster, 2001), 7.

4. Ibid., 90.

5. Ibid., 119.

6. D'Antonio, *Truth About Trump*, Kindle loc. 6156–60.

7. Blair, *The Trumps*, 226.

8. Tracie Rozhon, "Fred C. Trump, Postwar Master Builder of Housing for Middle Class, Dies at 93," *The New York Times*, June 26, 1999.

9. Trump and Schwartz, *Art of the Deal*, 96.

10. Blair, *The Trumps*, 231.

11. Trump and Schwartz, *Art of the Deal*, 79, 80.

12. Blair, *The Trumps*, 228.

13. D'Antonio, *Truth About Trump*, Kindle loc. 853.

14. Blair, *The Trumps*, 301.

15. Ibid.

16. Michael Kranish and Marc Fisher, *Trump Revealed: The Definitive Biography of the 45th President* (New York: Scribner, 2017), 18.

17. Ibid., 19.

18. Blair, *The Trumps*, 235.

19. Trump and Schwartz, *Art of the Deal*, 72.

20. D'Antonio, *Truth About Trump*, Kindle loc. 1287.

21. Blair, *The Trumps*, 233.

22. D'Antonio, *Truth About Trump*, Kindle loc. 986.

23. Ibid., Kindle loc. 988–90.

24. Ibid., Kindle loc. 981–83.

25. Ibid.

26. Ibid.

27. Kranish and Fisher, *Trump Revealed*, 27.

28. Ibid., 28.

29. Ibid., 25.

30. Ibid., 327.

Chapter 4 Killer

1. Johnston, *Making of Donald Trump*, Kindle loc. 386–88.

2. Arthur Goldwag, "Putting Donald Trump on the Couch," *The New York Times*, September 1, 2015.

3. Trump and Schwartz, *Art of the Deal*, 77.

4. Blair, *The Trumps*, 244.

5. Trump and Schwartz, *Art of the Deal*, 70.

6. Ibid.

7. Kranish and Fisher, *Trump Revealed*, 78.

8. Glenn Plaskin, "Playboy Interview: Donald Trump," *Playboy*, March 1990.

9. Trump and Schwartz, *Art of the Deal*, 71.

10. Ibid.

11. Kranish and Fisher, *Trump Revealed*, 77.

12. Ibid., 78.

13. Plaskin, "Playboy Interview: Donald Trump," as quoted in Blair, *The Trumps*, 320–21.

14. D'Antonio, *Truth About Trump*, Kindle loc. 6147.

15. Ibid., Kindle loc. 6145–46.

16. Trump and Schwartz, *Art of the Deal*, 98.

17. Ibid.

18. Ibid., 98–99.

19. Ibid., 100–101.

20. Tom Wolfe, "Dangerous Obsessions," *New York Times*, April 3, 1988, as quoted in D'Antonio, *Truth About Trump*, Kindle loc. 1603.

21. D'Antonio, *Truth About Trump*, Kindle loc. 218.

22. Johnston, *Making of Donald Trump*, Kindle loc. 415.

23. Ibid., Kindle loc. 351.

24. Ibid., Kindle loc. 357.

25. Ibid., Kindle loc. 362–63.

26. Ibid., Kindle loc. 385–88.

27. Blair, *The Trumps*, 262–63.

28. Trump and Schwartz, *Art of the Deal*, 58.

29. "Trump Says He Asks Dates to Take AIDS Test," *Saratoga Daily Gazette* (NY), June 29, 1991; Lori Brown, "Trump Plans for Safe Dating," *Austin American-Statesman*, June 29, 1991, as quoted in D'Antonio, *Truth About Trump*, Kindle loc. 4215.

Chapter 5 Peale

1. D'Antonio, *Truth About Trump*, Kindle loc. 6165–67.

2. *The Nation's Business*, August 1970, as quoted in Carol V. R. George, *God's Salesman: Norman Vincent Peale and the Power of Positive Thinking* (New York: Oxford University Press, 1993), 38.

3. George, *God's Salesman*, 30–31.

4. Norman Vincent Peale, "Department of Field Work Report, 1924," Boston University School of Theology, Norman Vincent Peale Manuscript Collection.

5. *Syracuse Post Standard*, May 25, 1931, as quoted in George, *God's Salesman*, 63.

6. Charles S. Braden, *Spirits in Rebellion: The Rise and Development of New Thought* (Dallas: Southern Methodist University Press, 1963), 391.

7. "Oprah Winfrey Show," February 7, 2007, as quoted in Janice Peck, *The Age of Oprah: Cultural Icon for the Neoliberal Era* (New York: Routledge, 2016), 212.

8. George, *God's Salesman*, 88.

9. Norman Vincent Peale, *You Can Win* (1938), preface, as quoted in Sidney Ahlstrom, *A Religious History of the American People* (New Haven: Yale University Press, 1972), 1033.

10. James Barron, "Overlooked Influences on Donald Trump: A Famous Minister and His Church," *The New York Times*, September 5, 2016.

11. *New York Sunday News*, December 11, 1955; William McLoughlin, *Revivals, Awakenings, and Reform* (New York: Ronald Press, 1959), as quoted in George, *God's Salesman*, 129.

12. Sidney Ahlstrom, *Religious History of the American People*, 1033.

13. Paul Johnson, *A History of the American People* (New York: Harper Collins, 1998), 839.

14. Alexis de Tocqueville, *Democracy in America*, vol. 2 (Cambridge: Sever and Francis, 1863), 154.

15. J. Gordon Melton, *The Encyclopedia of American Religions*, vol. 2 (Wilmington, NC: McGrath, 1978), 56, as quoted in George, *God's Salesman*, 134.

16. George, *God's Salesman*, 142–43.

17. "Interview with Norman Vincent Peale," July 6, 1989, Pawling, New York, as quoted in George, *God's Salesman*, 134.

18. John Sherrill, *Christian Life*, February 1970, as quoted in George, *God's Salesman*, 153.

19. George, *God's Salesman*, 131.

20. Ibid., 168.

21. *San Francisco Chronicle*, November 3, 1970, as quoted in George, *God's Salesman*, 214.

22. George, *God's Salesman*, 240.

23. Ibid.

Chapter 6 White

1. Katie Glueck, "Donald Trump's God Whisperer," *Politico*, July 11, 2016, http://www.politico.com/story/2016/07/donald-trump-pastor-paula-white-225315.

2. "Changing Colors, Changing Boundaries," *Ebony*, December 2004, 152–55.

3. Paula White, *He Loves Me He Loves Me Not: What Every Woman Needs to Know about Unconditional Love, But Is Afraid to Feel* (Orlando: Creation House, 1998), 113, as quoted in Shayne Lee and Phillip Luke Sinitiere, *Holy Mavericks: Innovational Motivators and the Spiritual Marketplace* (New York: New York University Press, 2009), 114.

4. Lee and Sinitiere, *Holy Mavericks*, 115.

5. White, *He Loves Me He Loves Me Not*, 76–77, as quoted in Lee and Sinitiere, *Holy Mavericks*, 116.

6. Gregory A. Smith and Jessica Martínez, "How the Faithful Voted: A Preliminary 2016 Analysis," PewResearch.org, November 9, 2016, http://www.pewresearch.org/fact-tank/2016/11/09/how-the-faithful-voted-a-preliminary-2016-analysis/.

7. Burke, "The Guilt-Free Gospel of Donald Trump."

8. Ibid.

9. Paula White, "Interview with Johnnie Moore," January 12, 2016, Washington, DC.

Chapter 7 Johnson

1. Politico staff, "Full Text: Trump Values Voter Summit Remarks," *Politico*, September 9, 2016, http://www.politico.com/story/2016/09/full-text-trump-values-voter-summit-remarks-227977.

2. Robert A. Caro, *Master of the Senate: The Years of Lyndon Johnson* (New York: Alfred A. Knopf, 2002), 546.

3. "Letter from Lyndon Johnson to J. R. Parten," June 3, 1954, LBJ Library, Dougherty, Dudley, June 1954 File.

4. For a description of the historical background to the 1934 amendment, see Wilfred R. Caron and Deirdre Dessingue, *IRC § 501(c)(3): Practical and Constitutional Implications of "Political" Activity Resolutions, 2 J.L. & Pol. 169* (1985), 185–87.

5. Cong. Rec. 9604 (1954).

6. Robert C. Albright, "Senate Votes Eisenhower Tax Revision Bill, 63 to 9," *Washington Post & Times Herald*, July 3, 1954.

7. Sandra Sobieraj, "Gore Team Campaigns through Midwest," *Associated Press*, November 6, 2000.

8. Dennis M. Mahoney, "Falwell Stumps for Bush at Church," *Columbus Dispatch*, November 6, 2000.

9. Steve Miller, "Hillary Courts Blacks at Church Services," *Washington Times*, November 6, 2000.

10. Glueck, "Trump's Religious Dealmaking Pays Dividends."

Chapter 8 Obama

1. Donald J. Trump, *Great Again: How to Fix Our Crippled America* (New York: Threshold Editions, 2016), Kindle loc. 1560.

2. Joseph Hartropp, "'God Will Use Us Well': The Profound Faith of Barack Obama," *Christian Today*, January 11, 2017, http://www.christiantoday.com/article/god.will.use.us.well.the.profound.faith.of.barack.obama/103781.htm.

3. Ed Pilkington, "Obama Angers Midwest Voters with Guns and Religion Remark," *The Guardian*, April 14, 2008.

4. "Hillary Clinton On Gay Rights Abroad: Secretary of State Delivers Historic LGBT Speech in Geneva," *The Huffington Post*, December 6, 2011.

5. Amina Kibrige, "Kenyan Muslim Clerics Fault Obama on Gay Marriage," *Africa Review*, May 12, 2012.

6. Eric J. Lyman, "Pope, Obama Visit Should be Cordial Despite Differences," *USA Today*, March 26, 2014.

Chapter 9 Hillary

1. Daniella Diaz, "Trump Calls Clinton 'a Nasty Woman'," *CNN Politics*, October 20, 2016, http://www.cnn.com/2016/10/19/politics/donald-trump-hillary-clinton-nasty-woman/.

2. Amy Chozick, "Hillary Clinton Calls Many Trump Backers 'Deplorables,' and G.O.P. Pounces," *The New York Times*, September 10, 2016.

3. Ashley Killough, "Trump: 'We Don't Know Anything about Hillary in Terms of Religion'," *CNN Politics*, June 22, 2016, http://www.cnn.com/2016/06/21/politics /donald-trump-hillary-clinton-religion/index.html.

4. "Faith and the 2016 Campaign," Pew Research Center: Religion & Public Life, January 27, 2016, http://www.pewforum.org/2016/01/27/faith-and-the-2016 -campaign/.

5. Hillary Rodham Clinton, *It Takes a Village* (New York: Simon & Schuster, 1996), 171.

6. Paul Kengor, *God and Hillary Clinton: A Spiritual Life* (New York: Harper Collins, 2007), 74.

7. Kenneth L. Woodward, "Soulful Matters," *Newsweek*, October 30, 1994, http://www.newsweek.com/soulful-matters-189302.

8. Michael McAuliff and Helen Kennedy, "Hil Has a Holy Cow over Immigrant Bill," *New York Daily News*, March 23, 2006, http://www.nydailynews.com /archives/news/hil-holy-immig-bill-article-1.576307.

9. Kengor, *God and Hillary Clinton*, 233.

10. Ibid., 210.

11. Ibid., 211.

12. Kevin Robillard, "Hillary Clinton Supports Gay Marriage," *Politico*, March 18, 2013, http://www.politico.com/story/2013/03/hillary-clinton-gay-marriage -support-088988.

13. Mark Hensch, "Clinton: 'Deep-Seated' Beliefs Block Abortion Access," *The Hill*, April 24, 2015, http://thehill.com/blogs/ballot-box/239974-clinton-deep-seated -beliefs-block-abortion-access.

14. Jesse Byrnes, "Hillary Clinton Defends Planned Parenthood Amid Video Controversy," *The Hill*, July 23, 2015, http://thehill.com/blogs/ballot-box/presi dential-races/249033-hillary-clinton-defends-planned-parenthood-amid-video.

Chapter 10 Voice

1. D'Antonio, *Truth About Trump*, Kindle loc. 6181–82.

2. Donald Trump, "Acceptance Speech at the RNC," VOX.com, July 22, 2016, http://www.vox.com/2016/7/21/12253426/donald-trump-acceptance-speech-trans cript-republican-nomination-transcript.

3. Blair, *The Trumps*, 8.

4. Ibid.

5. D'Antonio, *Truth About Trump*, Kindle loc. 6550.

6. Steve Pope, "Americans Living in Age of Profanity?," *USA Today*, March 28, 2006, http://usatoday30.usatoday.com/news/nation/2006-03-28-profanity_x.htm.

7. "Facts and Statistics about Infidelity," TruthAboutDeception.com, accessed March 1, 2017, https://www.truthaboutdeception.com/cheating-and-infidelity /stats-about-infidelity.html.

8. Toni Ridgaway, "Statistics Don't Tell the Whole Story When It Comes to Church Attendance," *Church Leaders*, October 7, 2013, http://churchleaders.com /pastors/pastor-articles/170739-statistics-don-t-tell-the-whole-story-when-it-comes -to-church-attendance.html.

9. Robert S. Feldman, "UMass Researcher Finds Most People Lie in Everyday Conversation," University of Massachusetts at Amherst, June 10, 2002, https://www.umass.edu/newsoffice/article/umass-amherst-researcher-finds-most-people-lie-everyday-conversation.

10. James Patterson, *The Day America Told the Truth: What People Really Believe about Everything That Really Matters* (Princeton, NY: Prentice-Hall, 1991), 48.

11. "The War on Marijuana in Black and White," ACLU, June 1, 2013, https://www.aclu.org/files/assets/aclu-thewaronmarijuana-rel2.pdf.

12. Jeff Nesbitt, "America, Racial Bias Does Exist," *U.S. News & World Report*, January 13, 2015, https://www.usnews.com/news/blogs/at-the-edge/2015/01/13/america-racial-bias-does-exist.

13. Timothy L. O'Brien, *Trump Nation: The Art of Being the Donald* (New York: Open Road Media, 2015), 31.

Chapter 11 The Art of Prophetic Distance, Part I

1. "Dwight Eisenhower to Honorable Arthur B. Langlie," August 11, 1952, PPF 1052, Graham, Billy; Box 966, White House Central Files-President's Personal File, Dwight D. Eisenhower Presidential Library, Abilene, Kansas.

2. "Billy Graham to Dwight D. Eisenhower," June 29, 1953, PPF 1052, Graham, Billy; Box 966, White House Central Files-President's Personal File, Dwight D. Eisenhower Presidential Library, Abilene, Kansas.

3. Billy Graham, *Just As I Am: The Autobiography of Billy Graham* (New York: HarperCollins, 1997), 442.

4. David Firestone, "Billy Graham Responds to Lingering Anger Over 1972 Remarks on Jews," *New York Times*, March 17, 2002, http://www.nytimes.com/2002/03/17/us/billy-graham-responds-to-lingering-anger-over-1972-remarks-on-jews.html.

5. Billy Graham, *Parade*, February 1, 1981.

6. As quoted in Jon Meacham, *American Gospel: God, the Founding Fathers, and the Making of a Nation* (New York: Random House, 2006), 215.

7. Jerry Falwell, *Strength for the Journey: An Autobiography* (New York: Simon & Schuster, 1987), 337.

8. Leviticus 19:15.

9. Luke 19:46.

10. Isaiah 56:7, emphasis added.

Chapter 12 The Art of Prophetic Distance, Part II

1. This story is taken with license from 1 Kings 22.

2. For more on this, see Joshua Wolf Schenk, *Lincoln's Melancholy: How Depression Challenged a President and Fueled His Greatness* (New York: Houghton Mifflin, 2005).

3. F. B. Carpenter, *The Inner Life of Abraham Lincoln: Six Months at the White House* (Lincoln: University of Nebraska Press, 1995), 117–19.

4. Sarah Pulliam Bailey, "Televangelist: Christians Who Don't Vote Are Going to Be Guilty of Murder," *Washington Post*, October 11, 2016, https://www.washington

post.com/news/acts-of-faith/wp/2016/10/11/televangelist-christians-who-dont-vote-are-going-to-be-guilty-of-murder/.

5. David Brody, "Exclusive: Michele Bachmann: 'God Raised Up' Trump to Be GOP Nominee," *CBN News*, August 30, 2016, http://www1.cbn.com/thebrodyfile/archive/2016/08/30/only-on-the-brody-file-michele-bachmann-says-god-raised-up-trump-to-be-gop-presidential-nominee.

6. "Rabbi Sees Donald Trump Ascendancy in Bible Codes: Signs of an American 'Cyrus the Great,'" WND.com, November 3, 2016, http://www.wnd.com/2016/11/rabbi-sees-donald-trump-ascendancy-in-bible-codes/.

7. "Many Americans Hear Politics from the Pulpit," Pew Research Center, Religion & Public Life, August 8, 2016, http://www.pewforum.org/2016/08/08/many-americans-hear-politics-from-the-pulpit/.

8. Max Lucado, "Does Donald Trump Pass the Civility Test?" *Christian Post*, February 26, 2016, http://www.christianpost.com/news/max-lucado-does-donald-trump-pass-the-decency-test-158679/.

9. Russell Moore, "A White Church No More," *New York Times*, May 6, 2016, https://www.nytimes.com/2016/05/06/opinion/a-white-church-no-more.html?_r=0.

10. Will Hall, "Texas Congregation Escrows CP over Concerns about Direction of SBC," *Baptist Message*, February 16, 2017, http://baptistmessage.com/26902-2/.

11. Herodotus, *The History of Herodotus*, vol. 1, trans. G. C. Macauley (London: MacMillan, 1890), December 1, 2008, http://www.gutenberg.org/files/2707/2707-h/2707-h.htm.

12. Isaiah 41:2.

13. Isaiah 44:28.

14. Isaiah 45:13.

15. Isaiah 45:1–3.

16. This story reproduced by permission. Author interview with Paul Marc Goulet, Nashville, Tennessee, February 9, 2017.

Epilogue

1. Lexington, "Trumpism Is Very Familiar to Europeans," *The Economist*, February 9, 2017, http://www.economist.com/news/united-states/21716649-what-donald-trump-has-common-marine-le-pen-and-geert-wilders-trumpism-very.

2. H. L. Mencken, *Baltimore Evening Sun*, July 26, 1920, as quoted in G. Jefferson Price III, "'The White House Will Be Adorned by a Downright Moron," *Baltimore Sun*, November 25, 2016, http://www.baltimoresun.com/news/opinion/oped/bs-ed-mencken-trump-20161119-story.html.

Appendix

1. Ryan Teague Beckwith, "Read President Trump's Remarks at the National Prayer Breakfast," *Time*, February 2, 2017, http://time.com/4658012/donald-trump-national-prayer-breakfast-transcript/.

2. "Presidential Candidate Donald Trump Remarks in Detroit," C-SPAN, September 3, 2016, https://www.c-span.org/video/?414743-1/donald-trump-speaks-africanamerican-church-detroit.

Bibliography

Ahlstrom, Sidney. *A Religious History of the American People.* New Haven: Yale University Press, 1972.

Bernstein, Carl. *A Woman in Charge.* New York: Alfred A. Knopf, 2007.

Blair, Gwenda. *The Trumps: Three Generations of Builders and a President.* New York: Simon & Schuster, 2015.

Byrne, Gary. *Crisis of Character: A White House Secret Service Officer Discloses His Firsthand Experience with Hillary, Bill, and How They Operate.* New York: Center Street, 2016.

Clinton, Hillary. *Living History.* New York: Simon & Schuster, 2003.

D'Antonio, Michael. *The Truth About Trump.* New York: St. Martin's Press, 2015, 2016.

Falwell, Jerry. *Strength for the Journey: An Autobiography.* New York: Simon & Schuster, 1987.

George, V. R. Carol. *God's Salesman: Norman Vincent Peale and the Power of Positive Thinking.* New York: Oxford University Press, 1993.

Gingrich, Newt, and Robert Reich. *Can Donald Trump Make America Great Again?* Toronto: House of Anansi Press, 2016.

Graham, Billy. *Just As I Am: The Autobiography of Billy Graham.* San Francisco: HarperSanFrancisco, 1997.

James, Aaron. *Assholes: A Theory of Donald Trump.* New York: Anchor Books, 2012.

Johnson, Paul. *A History of Christianity,* New York: MacMillan, 1976.

———. *A History of the American People.* New York: HarperCollins, 1997.

Johnston, David Cay. *The Making of Donald Trump*. Brooklyn: Melville House, 2016.

Kengor, Paul. *God and Hillary Clinton: A Spiritual Life*. New York: HarperCollins, 2007.

Kranish, Michael, and Marc Fisher. *Trump Revealed: The American Journey of Ambition, Ego, Money and Power*. New York: Scribner, 2017.

Lane, Christopher. *Surge of Piety: Norman Vincent Peale and the Remaking of American Religion*. New Haven: Yale University Press, 2016.

Mansfield, Stephen. *Ask the Question: Why We Must Demand Religious Clarity from Our Presidential Candidates*. Grand Rapids: Baker Books, 2016.

———. *The Faith of Barack Obama*. Nashville: Thomas Nelson, 2008.

———. *The Faith of George W. Bush*. New York: Jeremy Tarcher/Penguin, 2003.

Meacham, Jon. *American Gospel: God, the Founding Fathers, and the Making of a Nation*. New York: Random House, 2006.

O'Brien, Timothy L. *Trump Nation: The Art of Being the Donald*. New York: Open Road Media, 2015.

Moore, R. Laurence. *Religious Outsiders and the Making of Americans*. New York: Oxford University Press, 1986.

Moore, Russell. *Onward: Engaging the Culture without Losing the Gospel*. Nashville: B&H, 2015.

Neuhaus, Richard John. *Christian Faith and Public Policy: Thinking and Acting in the Courage of Uncertainty*. Minneapolis: Augsburg, 1977.

O'Donnell, John R., and James Rutherford. *Trumped! The Inside Story of the Real Donald Trump—His Cunning Rise and Spectacular Fall*. Hertford, NC: Crossroads Press, 2016.

Peale, Norman Vincent. *The Power of Positive Thinking: 10 Traits for Maximum Results*. New York: Touchstone, 2003.

Sheehy, Gail. *Hillary's Choice*. New York: Random House, 2000.

Sinitiere, Phillip Luke. *Holy Mavericks: Evangelical Innovators and the Spiritual Marketplace*. New York: NYU Press, 2009.

Solomon, Burt. *The Washington Century: Three Families and the Shaping of the Nation's Capital*. New York: HarperCollins, 2005.

Stockman, David. *Trumped: A Nation on the Brink of Ruin . . . And How to Bring It Back*. Baltimore: Laissez Faire Books, 2016.

Trump, Donald. *Great Again: How to Fix Our Crippled America*. New York: Simon & Schuster, 2015.

———. *Think Big: Make It Happen in Business and Life*. New York: HarperBusiness, 2008.

Trump, Donald, and Tony Schwartz. *The Art of the Deal*. New York: Random House, 1987.

Wallnau, Lance. *God's Chaos Candidate: Donald J. Trump and the American Unraveling*. Keller, TX: Killer Sheep Media, 2016.

Wear, Michael. *Reclaiming Hope*. Nashville: Thomas Nelson, 2017.

About the Author

Stephen Mansfield is a *New York Times* bestselling author whose works include *The Faith of George W. Bush*, *The Faith of Barack Obama*, *The Search for God and Guinness*, *The Character and Greatness of Winston Churchill*, *Lincoln's Battle with God*, and *Mansfield's Book of Manly Men*. He is a popular speaker who also leads a media training firm based in Washington, DC. Mansfield lives in Nashville, Tennessee, and his nation's capital with his wife, Beverly, who is an award-winning songwriter and producer. To learn more, visit StephenMansfield.TV.

★ ★ ★ ★ ★

CONNECT WITH
**STEPHEN
MANSFIELD**

STEPHENMANSFIELD.TV

 MansfieldWrites   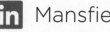 MansfieldWrites

 MansfieldWrites   MansfieldWrites

★ ★ ★ ★ ★

Connect with

BakerBooks

Relevant. Intelligent. Engaging.

Sign up for announcements about
new and upcoming titles at

www.bakerbooks.com/signup

 ReadBakerBooks

ReadBakerBooks

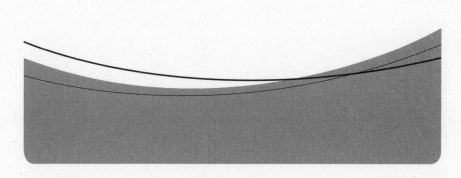